First World War
and Army of Occupation
War Diary
France, Belgium and Germany

3 DIVISION
7 Infantry Brigade
Royal Irish Rifles
2nd Battalion
4 August 1914 - 31 October 1915

WO95/1415/1

The Naval & Military Press Ltd
www.nmarchive.com
Published in association with The National Archives

Published by

The Naval & Military Press Ltd

Unit 10 Ridgewood Industrial Park,

Uckfield, East Sussex,

TN22 5QE England

Tel: +44 (0) 1825 749494

www.naval-military-press.com

www.nmarchive.com

This diary has been reprinted in facsimile from the original. Any imperfections are inevitably reproduced and the quality may fall short of modern type and cartographic standards.

© **Crown Copyright**
Images reproduced by permission of The National Archives, London, England, 2015.

Contents

Document type	Place/Title	Date From	Date To
Heading	WO95/1415 3 Div 7 Inf Bde 2 Btn Royal Irish Rifles Aug 1914-Oct 1915		
Heading	3rd Division 7th Infy Bde 2nd Battalion Royal Irish Rifles Aug-Dec 1914		
Heading	7th Brigade. 3rd Division. 2nd Battalion Royal Irish Rifles August 1914.		
War Diary	Tidworth	04/08/1914	13/08/1914
War Diary	Havre	14/08/1914	14/08/1914
War Diary	Rouen.	14/08/1914	14/08/1914
War Diary	Tidworth	13/08/1914	13/08/1914
War Diary	S' Hampton	14/08/1914	14/08/1914
War Diary	Rouen.	14/08/1914	16/08/1914
War Diary	Aumoye	16/08/1914	17/08/1914
War Diary	Marbaix	17/08/1914	20/08/1914
War Diary	St Hilaire	20/08/1914	21/08/1914
War Diary	Feignies	21/08/1914	22/08/1914
War Diary	Ciply.	22/08/1914	23/08/1914
War Diary	Nouvelles	23/08/1914	23/08/1914
War Diary	Harmignies	23/08/1914	24/08/1914
War Diary	La Bois Crette	25/08/1914	25/08/1914
War Diary	Maurois	26/08/1914	26/08/1914
War Diary	Caudry	26/08/1914	26/08/1914
War Diary	Beaurevoir	27/08/1914	27/08/1914
War Diary	Vermand	27/08/1914	27/08/1914
War Diary	Ham	28/08/1914	28/08/1914
War Diary	Tarlefesse	28/08/1914	30/08/1914
War Diary	Vic-Sur-Aisne	31/08/1914	31/08/1914
Miscellaneous	B Genl Bird General Remarks on the Tactics Aug. 1914	21/01/1913	21/01/1918
Miscellaneous	General Headquarters, Ireland, Parkgate, Dublin.	27/04/1920	27/04/1920
Miscellaneous	Mons File	01/05/1920	01/05/1920
Miscellaneous	With reference to the note on page 543 of the history of th Great war.		
Miscellaneous			
War Diary	Map Valenciennes	23/08/1914	25/08/1914
War Diary	Hand Passing numerous Bueoiacs along the the Inghy & Reumont roads	26/08/1914	20/09/1914
Diagram etc	General Binds Account		
Diagram etc	German Ed Gallary Rouge Maison Fm.		
Miscellaneous	Historical.	30/03/1931	30/03/1931
Miscellaneous	O.C. 1/Wilts. Regt.	29/03/1931	29/03/1931
Miscellaneous	O.C. 1/Wilts. Regt.	22/08/1914	22/08/1914
Miscellaneous	O.C. 1/Wilts. Regt.	29/03/1931	29/03/1931
Miscellaneous	O.C. 1/Wilts. Regt.	23/08/1914	23/08/1914
Miscellaneous	2nd Royal Irish Rifles and 1st Wilts. Bm. 67. 23rd.		
Miscellaneous	O.C. Wilts. BM 70.	23/08/1914	23/08/1914
Miscellaneous	1/Wilts.		
Miscellaneous	To H.Q. 1/Wilts.	23/08/1914	23/08/1914
Miscellaneous	O.C. Wilts.	29/03/1931	29/03/1931
Heading	7th Brigade. 3rd Division. 2nd Battalion Royal Irish Rifles September 1914		

War Diary	Coyolles	01/09/1914	01/09/1914
War Diary	Villers	02/09/1914	02/09/1914
War Diary	Pringy	02/09/1914	03/09/1914
War Diary	La Marche	03/09/1914	03/09/1914
War Diary	Sancy	04/09/1914	04/09/1914
War Diary	Chatres	05/09/1914	06/09/1914
War Diary	Faremoutiers	07/09/1914	07/09/1914
War Diary	Les Petits Aulnois	07/09/1914	07/09/1914
War Diary	Bussieres	08/09/1914	09/09/1914
War Diary	Bezu	10/09/1914	10/09/1914
War Diary	Grand Rozoy	11/09/1914	12/09/1914
War Diary	Cerseuil	13/09/1914	13/09/1914
War Diary	Braine	13/09/1914	14/09/1914
War Diary	Valley of Aisne	15/09/1914	22/09/1914
War Diary	Augy	22/09/1914	26/09/1914
War Diary	Chassemy	27/09/1914	28/09/1914
War Diary	Braine	28/09/1914	30/09/1914
War Diary	Couvrelles	01/10/1914	01/10/1914
Miscellaneous	Copy of Letters Addressed to Wing Commander Slessor.		
Heading	7th Brigade. 3rd Division. 2nd Battalion Royal Irish Rifles. October 1914		
War Diary	Couvrelles	01/10/1914	01/10/1914
War Diary	Grand Rozoy	02/10/1914	02/10/1914
War Diary	Noroy	03/10/1914	03/10/1914
War Diary	Vaumoise	04/10/1914	04/10/1914
War Diary	Verberie	05/10/1914	06/10/1914
War Diary	Noyelles	06/10/1914	07/10/1914
War Diary	Le Plessiel	08/10/1914	08/10/1914
War Diary	Regnauville	09/10/1914	09/10/1914
War Diary	Floringhem	10/10/1914	10/10/1914
War Diary	Pernes	11/10/1914	11/10/1914
War Diary	Hinges.	11/10/1914	12/10/1914
War Diary	Lacouture	12/10/1914	13/10/1914
War Diary	Near Croix Barbee	14/10/1914	15/10/1914
War Diary	Near Rouge Croix	16/10/1914	16/10/1914
War Diary	Bois De Biez	17/10/1914	17/10/1914
War Diary	L'Aventure	17/10/1914	18/10/1914
War Diary	Bois De Biez	19/10/1914	20/10/1914
War Diary	L'Aventure	20/10/1914	21/10/1914
War Diary	Halpegarbe	21/10/1914	21/10/1914
War Diary	Neuve Chapelle	22/10/1914	27/10/1914
War Diary	Richebourg St Vaast	28/10/1914	29/10/1914
War Diary	La Couture	30/10/1914	30/10/1914
War Diary	Merris	31/10/1914	31/10/1914
Miscellaneous	2nd Bn Royal Irish Rifles		
Miscellaneous	Major R.A.C. Daunt. D.S.O.	22/06/1915	22/06/1915
Miscellaneous	Adjutant 2/R.I. Rifles	28/06/1915	28/06/1915
Miscellaneous	Major R.A.C. Daunt D.S.O.	16/07/1915	16/07/1915
Heading	7th Brigade. 3rd Division. 2nd Battalion Royal Irish Rifles. November 1914		
War Diary	Locre (Belgium)	01/11/1914	04/11/1914
War Diary	Hooge	05/11/1914	20/11/1914
War Diary	Westoutre	21/11/1914	26/11/1914
War Diary	Locre	27/11/1914	30/11/1914

Heading	7th Brigade. 3rd Division. 2nd Battalion Royal Irish Rifles. December 1914		
War Diary	Kemmel	01/12/1914	03/12/1914
War Diary	Westoutre	04/12/1914	06/12/1914
War Diary	Locre	07/12/1914	09/12/1914
War Diary	Kemmel	10/12/1914	12/12/1914
War Diary	Locre	13/12/1914	15/12/1914
War Diary	Kemmel	16/12/1914	18/12/1914
War Diary	Locre	19/12/1914	27/12/1914
War Diary	Westoutre	28/12/1914	31/12/1914
Heading	3rd Division 7th Infy Bde 2nd Battalion Royal Irish Rifles. Jan-Oct 1915 To 25 Division 74 Brigade		
Map	Voormezeele		
Heading	7th Inf. Bde. 3rd Div. War Diary 2nd Battn. The Royal Irish Rifles. January 1915		
War Diary	Westoutre	01/01/1915	04/01/1915
War Diary	Kemmel	05/01/1915	08/01/1915
War Diary	Westoutre	09/01/1915	12/01/1915
War Diary	Kemmel	13/01/1915	16/01/1915
War Diary	Locre	17/01/1915	20/01/1915
War Diary	Kemmel	21/01/1915	24/01/1915
War Diary	Westoutre	25/01/1915	28/01/1915
War Diary	Kemmel	29/01/1915	31/01/1915
Heading	7th Inf. Bde. 3rd Div. War Diary 2nd Battn. The Royal Irish Rifles. February 1915		
War Diary	Kemmel	01/02/1915	01/02/1915
War Diary	Locre	02/02/1915	05/02/1915
War Diary	Kemmel	06/02/1915	09/02/1915
War Diary	Westoutre	10/02/1915	13/02/1915
War Diary	Kemmel	14/02/1915	22/02/1915
War Diary	Westoutre	23/02/1915	26/02/1915
War Diary	Kemmel	27/02/1915	28/02/1915
Heading	7th Inf. Bde. 3rd Div. War Diary 2nd Battn. The Royal Irish Rifles. March 1915		
War Diary	Kemmel	01/03/1915	04/03/1915
War Diary	Westoutre	05/03/1915	13/03/1915
War Diary	Dranoutre	14/03/1915	14/03/1915
War Diary	Westoutre	15/03/1915	16/03/1915
War Diary	Locre	17/03/1915	17/03/1915
War Diary	Kemmel	18/03/1915	23/03/1915
War Diary	La Clytte	24/03/1915	29/03/1915
War Diary	Elzenwalle	30/03/1915	31/03/1915
Heading	7th Inf. Bde. 3rd Div. War Diary 2nd Battn. The Royal Irish Rifles. April 1915		
War Diary	Elzenwalle H.36 C	01/04/1915	04/04/1915
War Diary	La Clytte (N.7.C)	05/04/1915	10/04/1915
War Diary	Vierstraat area N.12 d	11/04/1915	16/04/1915
War Diary	Dickebusch	17/04/1915	20/04/1915
War Diary	Vierstraat area N.12 d	21/04/1915	25/04/1915
War Diary	Dickebusch	26/04/1915	30/04/1915
Heading	7th Inf. Bde. 3rd Div. War Diary 2nd Battn. The Royal Irish Rifles. May 1915		
War Diary	Vierstraat area N 12 d	01/05/1915	05/05/1915
War Diary	Dickebusch	06/05/1915	06/05/1915
War Diary	Ypres	07/05/1915	07/05/1915
War Diary	Ypres N2 Hill 60	08/05/1915	11/05/1915

War Diary	Laclytte Dickebusch	12/05/1915	12/05/1915
War Diary	Laclytte	13/05/1915	16/05/1915
War Diary	Vierstraat area N.12 d	17/05/1915	20/05/1915
War Diary	Dickebusch	21/05/1915	24/05/1915
War Diary	Vierstraat area (N.12 d)	25/05/1915	31/05/1915
Heading	7th Inf. Bde. 3rd Div. War Diary 2nd Battn. The Royal Irish Rifles. June 1915		
War Diary	Vierstraat area (N.12 d)	01/06/1915	30/06/1915
Heading	7th Inf. Bde. 3rd Div. War Diary 2nd Battn. The Royal Irish Rifles. July 1915		
War Diary		01/07/1915	31/07/1915
Heading	7th Inf. Bde. 3rd Div. War Diary 2nd Battn. The Royal Irish Rifles. August 1915		
War Diary		01/08/1915	01/09/1915
Heading	7th Inf. Bde. 3rd Div. War Diary 2nd Battn. The Royal Irish Rifles. September 1915		
War Diary		01/09/1915	30/09/1915
Diagram etc	Hooge and Bellewarde Lake		
Heading	D.A. War Diary 21 R. Irish Rifles August 1914 Sept. 1914 Respectively		
Heading	7th Inf. Bde. 3rd Div. Battn. Transferred with Bde. to 25th Div. 18.10.15. Battn. Transferred to 74th Inf. Bde. 25th Div. 26.10.15. War Diary 2nd Battn. The Royal Irish Rifles. October 1915		
War Diary		01/10/1915	31/10/1915

WO95/1415

3 DIV 7 INF BDE

2 Btn ROYAL IRISH RIFLES
Aug 1914 – Oct 1915

3RD DIVISION
7TH INFY BDE

2ND BATTALION
ROYAL IRISH RIFLES
AUG - DEC 1914

7th Brigade.
3rd Division.

2nd BATTALION

ROYAL IRISH RIFLES

AUGUST 1 9 1 4.

WAR DIARY
or
INTELLIGENCE SUMMARY.
(Erase heading not required.)

Army Form C. 2118.

Instructions regarding War Diaries and Intelligence Summaries are contained in F.S. Regs., Part II. and the Staff Manual respectively. Title pages will be prepared in manuscript.

Hour, Date, Place	Summary of Events and Information	Remarks and references to Appendices
6 p.m. 4.VIII.14 Tidworth	Batt. ordered to mobilize.	
5.VIII.14 to 9.VIII.14 "	Batt. mobilizes in accordance with Batt. Scheme.	
	Mobilization complete.	
2.30 p.m. 13.VIII.14 Tidworth	1st Train with ½ Batt. entrained for SOUTHAMPTON — arrived 5 p.m. embarked on board S.S. ENNISFALLEN — sailed from SOUTHAMPTON	
5 a.m. 14.VIII.14 Havre	9 p.m. Reached HAVRE about 5 a.m. next day — sailed up the	
7.30 p.m. " " Rouen.	River SEINE — Reached ROUEN 7.30 p.m. men disembarked & marched to Rest Camp at MONT ST. AIGNAN: where the other half Batt. was met.	
3.30 p.m. 13.VIII.14 Tidworth	2nd Train, with ½ Batt. entrains for SOUTHAMPTON — arrived 6 p.m.	
4.15 a.m. 14.VIII.14 S'hampton	Embarked on board S.S. SARNIA — sailed from SOUTHAMPTON 4.15 a.m. next morning. Arrived ROUEN at 6 p.m. without touching at HAVRE	
6.0 p.m. " " Rouen.	marches to Rest Camp at MONT ST. AIGNAN — where was met by other half Batt.	
15.VIII.14 Rouen	Remained in Rest Camp — weather very wet — said camp soon became impassable	
7.30 a.m. 16.VIII.14 Rouen	Batt. entrains at ROUEN for AUMOYE via AMIENS — arrived thro'	
10.15 p.m. " " Aumoye	10.15 p.m. Billeted in a township 1½ miles from station. (Chesni Monrant)	
6.45 a.m. 17.VIII.14 Aumoye	Marched in Brigade to MARBAIX — arrived about 12 noon & billeted	
12 noon " " Marbaix	Billets.	

WAR DIARY
or
INTELLIGENCE SUMMARY.
(Erase heading not required.)

Army Form C. 2118.

Instructions regarding War Diaries and Intelligence Summaries are contained in F. S. Regs., Part II. and the Staff Manual respectively. Title pages will be prepared in manuscript.

Hour, Date, Place	Summary of Events and Information	Remarks and references to Appendices
18.VIII.14 MARBAIX	Remained in billets – a route march was carried out in the morning. It was found half certain amusements were necessary to ensure proper discipline. I.C. Kit & Arm Rations parade at Ruville. Followed by washing & water filling parades – an early turn each day at Battn H.Q.	
19.VIII.14 "	Remained in billets – a MG march was carried out in the morning. The weather was hot. While in these billets posts on all roads were found by the Regiments of the Bde. The posts found by the Battn saw nothing of an unusual nature.	
8 a.m. 20.VIII.14 MARBAIX	Left billets for first move at ST HILAIRE at 8 a.m. – which was occupied in conjunction with the S. Lancashire Regt. In the afternoon carried out a Bde Route march.	
" ST HILAIRE	Marching to AVESNES – where the inhabitants gave the Bde a great ovation. The march was a short one but owing to the heat being fearfully high this was little done. The men appeared to feel the heat.	
1.30 a.m. 21.VIII.14 St HILAIRE	Orders received from H.Q. 7th Inf. Bde. to join the Bde at ST AUBIN, the march to first billets at FEIGNIES via MAUBEUGE. The total distance was about 17 miles. The men appeared ten exhausted – this may have been due	
3.30 p.m. 21.VIII.14 FEIGNIES	to the early start (4.45 a.m.) & the fact that was = Inf. were nearby till 3.30 p.m. The resulting in delay in the preparation of the mens dinners – which was not had till 8 p.m. The usual small posts was found on the roads leading to Villebury area.	
3.30 a.m. 22.VIII.14 FEIGNIES	Orders received at 3.30 p.m. that the Battn was ordered to march at 8.47 a.m. about an hour later the hour of parade was put forward an a half hour. The Bn marched to QUEVY LE PETIT when the troops comprising the column 1.2. 7th Inf. Bde & 42^A F.A. Bde. 57th Coy R.E. & Sect^n F. Amb^t halted for about 2 hours. The march was then continued with heavy dust.	
3 p.m. CIPLY.	tracks to CIPLY – these billets were taken up about 3 p.m. CIPLY is a small industrial village. Part 100 inhabitants & his about 2 miles due S. of MONS. The middle of the day was very hot and sultry. Several aeroplanes were observed circling over CIPLY but it was impossible to say whether they were friendly or hostile.	

WAR DIARY or INTELLIGENCE SUMMARY.

Army Form C. 2118.

(Erase heading not required.)

Instructions regarding War Diaries and Intelligence Summaries are contained in F. S. Regs., Part II. and the Staff Manual respectively. Title pages will be prepared in manuscript.

Hour, Date, Place	Summary of Events and Information	Remarks and references to Appendices
2 am 23-VIII/IX-14 CIPLY	Reveille 2am orders to march at 4.30 am but Battn did not move off till 7am. Marched a short distance beyond NOUVELLES — halted. Marched about half way back to CIPLY.	
2 pm 23-VIII/IX-14 NOUVELLES	At 2 pm marched to HARMIGNIES where received a report that some of the 15th Hussars had been forced back. Sent forward 2 coys of re-infore. Royal Scots on their	
3.45 pm 23-VIII/IX-14 HARMIGNIES	hill about HARMIGNIES, commenced entrenching when enemy's artillery opened, about 3.45 pm. C & D coys in firing line. A + B coys in reserve on GIVRY MONS road. These latter coys were afterwards brought up to prolong the line on the left, occupying trenches near the road. D Coy was somewhat separated filling up a gap between two coys of Royal Scots. Enemy attacked with infantry covered by artillery and cav: with one machine gun on their left. Bewailed 4 killed, wounded.	
1.30 am 24-VIII/IX-14 HARMIGNIES	Orders received to withdraw A + B coys withdrew at 1.30 am D Coy 2 am. Battn assembled at NOUVELLES. Orders were given to leave packs, extra ammunition and the picks & shovels, which had been carried down from the trenches, were to be abandoned.	

Army Form C. 2118

WAR DIARY
or
INTELLIGENCE SUMMARY.
(Erase heading not required.)

Instructions regarding War Diaries and Intelligence Summaries are contained in F. S. Regs., Part II. and the Staff Manual respectively. Title pages will be prepared in manuscript.

Hour, Date, Place	Summary of Events and Information	Remarks and references to Appendices
24-VIII-14	Retired vid MALADRIE – QUÉVY – BAVAI – ST WAAST to LA BOIS CRETTE and took up outpost position.	
25-VIII-14 LA BOIS CRETTE	Took up position covering the retirement; subsequently the Battn acted as rearguard to the Brigade. Retired via GOMMEGNIES – LE QUESNOY. At LE QUESNOY received report that a strong German force of all arms was in our rear. Fell back to ROMERIES and LE CATEAU.	
26-VIII-14 MAUROIS	to MAUROIS and went into temporary billets	
26-VIII-14 CAUDRY	Received orders to take up a position near CAUDRY. Battle of CAUDRY, following casualties occurred. Major Charley, 2/Lts Clark, 2/Lt Matthews – Donaldson, 2/Lt F.L. Finlay and 29 other ranks wounded. 2/Lt F.L. Finlay and 29 other ranks wounded. 6 other ranks killed. Fell back in the evening to BEAUREVOIR	Attached infant from Reff also Lr recruit of Lt Feu was written
2 am 27-VIII-14 BEAUREVOIR	Continued the retirement to VERMAND halting four hours on the way at HARGICOURT.	
9 p.m. 27-VIII-14 VERMAND	Halted at VERMAND for &, continued the retirement at 9 p.m. to HAM arriving there at 4 a.m. Continued	
4 am 28-VIII-14 HAM	the march to TARLEFESSE arriving about 3 p.m.	
3 p.m. 28-VIII-14 TARLEFESSE	& went on into billets	

Army Form C. 2118.

WAR DIARY
or
INTELLIGENCE SUMMARY.
(Erase heading not required.)

Instructions regarding War Diaries and Intelligence Summaries are contained in F. S. Regs., Part II. and the Staff Manual respectively. Title pages will be prepared in manuscript.

Hour, Date, Place	Summary of Events and Information	Remarks and references to Appendices
1pm 29-VIII-14 TARLEFESSE	Left about 1pm & took up a position in the rear about Bois D'AUTRECOURT. On outpost in the woods all night.	
30-VIII-14	Marched in early morning via MORLINCOURT VARESNES and rejoined Brigade at PONTOISE. Marched to VIC-SUR-AISNE & went into billets.	
31-VIII-14 VIC-SUR-AISNE	Marched from VIC-SUR-AISNE about 8.30 am via MONTIGNY - VILLERS-COTTERETS TO COYOLLES. Two companies C.& D. on outpost, remainder of Batt. bivouac.	

B. Genl Bird's General Remarks
on the Tactics of Aug. 1914

11 Evelyn Mansions
Carlisle Place
London S.W.1
21. 1. 18.

Dear Atkinson

Enclosed are notes on what I can recollect of the movements of my battalion during the retreat & subsequent advance to the Aisne.

My memory is not clear as to our halting places before reaching Meaux and after the Marne. I may also have put events on 16th, 17th & 18th September in wrong chronological order.

One got so little sleep during the retreat & advance, when at best orders came in at midnight or a little earlier, & reveille was at 4 A.M., & physically one was tired with marching, that the names of some of the smaller halting places reached at dusk & left at dawn have escaped me.

Our pre-war text books erred, I think, only in that the possibility of close fighting in long drawn out battles, such as occurred in the Russo-Japanese war, was not sufficiently considered. We were convinced that in well developed Europe a war of movement would be fought, because, if for no other reason, the Germans seemed to contemplate this, & in addition most economists scouted the idea of a long drawn out struggle. Moreover there was the feeling that the dash of our men would be lowered were they taught in peace the slow methods of trench warfare.

In principle, I think our system of holding a series of localities in a defensive position, and not a long continuous line was correct. But it was not sufficiently understood that covered communications between the localities and from them to the rear were also necessary

Within my brief experience the very extensive frontages taken up, which left no troops available as reserves, prevented our principles from being put into practice as regards counterattack.

So little time, also, was available for entrenchment when we did stand to fight, that, as a rule, villages which seemed to afford some cover, were selected as our "localities". As a result the enemy's artillery was afforded a series of good targets on which fire could be & was concentrated, & our men, who perhaps were somewhat crowded in the villages, suffered accordingly.

Speaking for myself it seemed to me that our means of intercommunication & arrangements for distribution of information were at fault.
During the retreat & advance I never knew the general position of our cavalry brigades or of neighbouring infantry divisions; nor had I any idea as to our general intentions at Mons, the Marne or the Aisne; or before & after Le Cateau. I do not know whether it was my fault or that of the brigade that I lost touch with them on 24th, 25th & 26th, but I had only 3 or 4 cyclists & my adjutant & senior major available for communication, since for some reason visual signalling was rarely used. I have an idea that the signalling kit of the brigade signal section was lost.

In two items of prewar preparation our system was fully vindicated – viz marching and rapid fire. The Germans never stood up to our rapid fire for more than a quarter of an hour, & we could not have done the retreat & advance had not march discipline been well taught in peace.

Speaking with diffidence it seemed to me that more might have been done by our artillery to help us.

I do not think we had any artillery cooperation at Mons, & little or none at the Aisne — I mean my battalion. If artillery officers had come up to our positions & consulted with us this would have been righted.

The dreadful congestion of traffic that occurred at first in all billeting areas during the retreat was a serious danger & would have been disastrous had we been really hard pressed. After we passed Noyon matters improved in this respect.

German tactics in attack appeared very like our own, in principle.
They seemed to make deliberate preparation before launching an attack, bringing up guns & infantry onto the ground.
The artillery preparation then began more or less simultaneously along the front of attack, & where it was thought sufficient effect had been produced the infantry came on with all available machine guns.
If the infantry attack did not succeed it was at once abandoned & more preparation commenced.
The German position on the Aisne was good. Their artillery commanded the flat marshy valley, all bridges were broken so that our guns could not cross, & as a result when our infantry occupied the southern edges of the bluffs on the north of the valley they found themselves without artillery support, close to entrenched infantry who could not be reached by our guns, & exposed to the full force of hostile artillery fire. The Germans, then, gained the time they required to bring up reinforcements, & when they arrived were able to attack in advantageous circumstances.
The positions of the German infantry were selected to afford concealment & avoid fire, the field of fire from the trenches was restricted & they relied mainly on flanking

machine gun and oblique field gun fire to beat off our attacks. Placed at the foot of a slope the Germans, however, suffered the usual drawback of difficulty of reinforcement & also of bringing up food & ammunition.

At first the Germans burst their shrapnel high & did little harm, nor was their fire accurate. At the Aisne, however, the bursts were good, but, even so, little damage was done in proportion to the ammunition expended

The H.E. was hardly more effective, that is the small shell fired at us.

I thought the German pursuit slack & cautious. They ought to have taken my battalion on two if not three occasions.

Apparently they did not march until late in the day — about noon — possibly owing to difficulties as to supplies, & as a result they only came up with us at nightfall, & we always made good our escape during darkness.

I have only one other item to mention — the dreadful saltness of the bully beef. After eating it an unquenchable thirst resulted which was very trying to men making long marches in hot weather & in a not too well watered country.

Believe me
Yours Sincerely
W. D. Bird.

The maps are in another envelope with our routes marked in green.

GENERAL HEADQUARTERS, IRELAND,
PARKGATE,
DUBLIN.

27. 4. 20.

Dear General,

I'm afraid I'm a bit foggy concerning the facts you ask about but this is what I _think_ happened though I can't absolutely swear to it.

About 8 p.m. we received a message that you were to go & meet General Doran at once to discuss the situation. You went alone & on coming back told me we were to start at midnight or 1 a.m. (I forget the exact hour) and try and rejoin the 7th Brigade who would probably be at NOUVELLES (near CIPLY, the village we'd spent the night before in) The impression I gained was that General Doran had communicated with the 7th Brigade and that they were the wishes of Genl. McCracken. As far as I recollect you received your orders personally from General Doran & acting in writing. I also remember being under the impression at the time that the idea of the retirement was to get out of the shell trap we were in; join up with the 7th Brigade again; let the Hun go on shelling the vacated position and if an opportunity came to be ready to counter attack him from the vicinity of NOUVELLES. Of course this latter idea may have been all wrong but that was my impression at the time.

About 5 a.m. or perhaps a bit earlier we got near NOUVELLES & you sent me on ahead to see if any one of the 7th Brigade Staff were there. There wasn't a soul in the village so the Battalion moved on to CIPLY, & I think you then decided to march in the direction of MAUBERGE. It was about this time that we got rid of most of our kits. I remember clearly your expecting someone of the 7 Brigade Staff to be at NOUVELLES or CIPLY & that when no one was there that we were "in the air" as regards orders & everything else. Also the Hun was beginning to work round with our flanks apparently.

Mons file

2/R.I.Rif/7/3

1.5.20.

Dear Edmonds

I enclose a letter from my adjutant re Mons. This has stimulated my memory as follows:

At about 8 P.M. I was discussing with G. Morris the advisability of making a counter-attack at dawn, when a message arrived (from?) directing me to fall back in succession after Doran's brigade.

I sent an officer to communicate with Doran, & others to reconnoitre our line of retirement.

Doran replied summoning me to his

H.Q. I cycled there, in consequence, at about 10 P.M.

It was then arranged that we should be ready to retire at midnight, but should not move until orders were received from Doran. These arrived at about 2 A.M.

We went to Rouvelles, because we hoped to find the 7th brigade there. Actually we found our 1st line transport only.

We did not fall back on Maubeuge because I saw Bucé-Davies (G.S.O 3 of 5ᵗ Div?) & found out from him the whereabouts of the 3rd division.

We marched across country in the direction of Bavai, & eventually struck a road on which F. Maurice was driving in a car, & he gave us definite orders.

Yours Sincerely

W D Bird

(Then Commanding 2/R. Ir Rgt.
7th Inf Brigade)

With reference to the Note on page 542 of the History of the Great War, France and Belgium, Vol I, 1933, the following are the routes taken by, and the approximate distances traversed by, the 2nd Battalion The Royal Irish Rifles of the 7th Infantry Brigade from the 24th to the 30th August, 1914, both dates inclusive.

24th August: Left position in area between Harmignies and B[...] at 2AM, marched via Nouvelles – Noirchain – Ge[...] Hon – Bavai, where rejoined the Brigade, – St [...] and went on outpost duty. 16 miles.

25th August: Battalion rearguard of 7th Infantry Brigade. St Waas[...] – Le Quesnoy – Romeries – Beaurain – Ovillers – Monta[...] – Le Cateau, marched through the central square – Reumont – Maurois, billets at about 3.45AM on 26th. 30 miles.

26th August: Maurois – Bertry – railway south of Audencourt – Tronquoy – Caudry – Tronquoy – Clary – Elincourt – Serain – Poncheux – Beaurevoir. 18 miles.

27th August: Battalion rearguard of 7th Brigade. Beaurevoir – Bellicourt – Hargecourt – Jeancourt – Vendelles – Soyecourt, in touch with 4th Division, – Vermand. 16 miles.

27/28th August: Vermand to Tarlefesse, north of Noyon. 26 miles.

29/30th August: On outpost duty 1PM in the forest north of Silency. Fell back 2AM, 30th August, crossed Oise 6AM at Varennes. Marched 3 or 4 miles and then remained for about 6 hours on a waterless down somewhere near Cuts. Marched to Vic sur Aisne. About 17 miles

On Aug. 26th B Coy & ½ A Coy were sent into CAUDRY under command of Capt. Master — the orders were to proceed to the market square and to await instructions. On arrival in the market-square the town was heavily bombarded, several men were killed and wounded and many knocked down by the violence of the explosions. In order to escape the bombardment the men were pushed forward to the Northern edge of the town, where an entrenched position was taken up, here the detachment got in touch with the Worcestershire Regt. on the left and mixed detachments on the right. In this position the detachment came under the fire of about 1 Batt'n of German Infantry with several machine guns, and also under shrapnel fire, the latter very slowly damaged. About 2 PM Capt. Master received an order from Sgt. Gibson of the Royal Irish Regt., that as the troops on the right had retired from the village he was to retire also. Capt. Master had this order confirmed and the retirement was carried out under the direction of the Major of the Royal Irish Regt.

During the retirement Capt. Master was requested to guard the 30th Howitzer Brigade R.F.A. he halted and reported his intention to the O.C. 2/M Regt and asked for instructions before a reply was received the general retirement began. The detachment covered the retirement of the 30th Bde R.F.A. and certain stragglers and subsequently retired and joined the rest of the Batt'n and formed part of the rearguard to the 3rd Division.

Owing to the scattered state of the troops in the town it is impossible to make a complete list of the casualties but the following is as near as can be ascertained

Notes in regard to the movements of the 2nd
R.I. Rifles from 23.8.14 to 19.9.14.
by B. Genl W.D. Bird. D.S.O. then comm'd'g the battalion

Night of 22/23rd August the battalion was in
billets at CIPLY, except B company on
outpost duty.

23rd Aug
Map
Valenciennes

On 23rd the battalion stood to arms at 4.30 A.M.
At about 6 A.M. I was sent for by the brigadier,
B.Genl McCracken, & in company with him
& his brigade major rode, I think, to HARMIGNIES.
I was then ordered to bring up and entrench my
battalion on a very extended frontage from
HARMIGNIES to a high bluff, probably BOIS LA
HAUT.

As we were moving into position we met some
Guardsmen of 2nd division who said they had
come to relieve us, & soon afterwards orders
were received from brigade headquarters to
withdraw, I think, to the cross roads at the S
of NOUVELLES & go into reserve.

This point was reached at about 11.30 A.M. &
arms were piled.

Between 12.30 P.M. & 1 P.M. the divisional squadron
of 3rd division came galloping back from the
front & the men said that they had lost heavily
& that the Germans were advancing.

The battalion was fallen in & extended & while
this was taking place Major Duncan of the
Royal Scots rode up & informed me that
we had been detailed to reinforce the 9th (?)
B.Genl Doran's brigade & were to move forward
& occupy the bluff mentioned above.

Guided by Major Duncan the battalion reached
its position at about 2.30 P.M.

Here one company of R. Scots was found entrenched on ground where, owing to its convex shape, the effective field of fire was limited to about 300ˣ.

The remainder of the R Scots were entrenched generally along the GIVRY-MONS road a some 300ˣ-400ˣ further back than the company on the bluff.

Two companies of the 2 R.I.R were ordered to occupy & entrench the bluff, cooperating with the company of R Scots, & the remaining companies placed in a deep cutting where the road ascends the bluff.

R Scots

M Guns R I Rifles   R Scots

R I Rifles

The company flanking the position of the R Scots & the machine guns had a good field of fire for about 1000ˣ, the other company a poor field of fire, the ground from about 1500ˣ - 1000ˣ being dead.

R I Rifles

3.

While the two companies on the bluff were entrenching a German battery was located about 2000x to the front & this was reported to the commander of our nearest artillery brigade who, however, did not engage it.

The German attack began at about 4 P.M, & just before or after this I received a message from Lt Col McMicking commanding R Scots that unless he received two companies he did not think he could hold his ground. The two reserve companies of the R.I. Rifles were therefore sent to Lt Col McMicking & report made to B/Genl McCracken as to the situation.

The German attack developed on the lines usually practised in 1914. Owing to the contour of the ground the enemy attacking the bluff were invisible from about 1500x until they closed to 300x, where they were checked.

The company flanking the position of the main body of the R Scots, & the machine guns, however, caused a good many casualties in the troops attacking the R. Scots.

The enemy's artillery fire was fairly heavy, shrapnel only being used. The bursts, however, were high and accuracy poor, a good many shell bursting in the trees which lined the MONS road.

Between 5 & 5.30 P.M. we were joined by a battalion of Grenadier Guards under Lt Col Drummond (?) & one of Irish Guards under Lt Col G. Morris

At nightfall the Germans brought up six machine guns, and made an attempt to advance but relinquished it as soon as our rapid fire was opened. I think they then fell back to cook, leaving an outpost line opposite to us.

4.

At about 7.30 P.M. touch was obtained with a company of 2nd division on the lower part of the bluff on our right.

Between 8 P.M. & 8.30 P.M. an order was received from B.Genl McCracken that we were to fall back at 10 P.M. & I at once sent an officer to reconnoitre the route to the point from which we had advanced, where the bulk of our 1st line transport had been left.

A report was also sent to B.Genl Doran who thereupon directed me not to withdraw until orders came from him to do so.

On receipt of these instructions I bicycled about 1½ miles down the road towards MONS & saw B.Genl Doran who informed me that I was to hold the bluff until his brigade had withdrawn & was then to retire. He estimated that I should be able to move at about midnight.

During the early part of the night the Guards received orders from Lord Cavan not to leave the bluff. As they were under me & I was under B.Genl Doran, I however directed them to conform to my movements. A full report of this was made to B.Genl McCracken in writing on evening of 24th.

24th Aug

Actually we got away at about 2 A.M., leaving the Guards to cover our retirement & then to follow, & picking up the company of R. Scots that was on the bluff & the company of the 2nd division the battalion reached the S of NOUVELLES at about 4.30 A.M. - 5 A.M. Here we found the remainder of our 1st line transport.

After getting under cover I sent the senior major & adjutant to try & find the brigade headquarters but without avail, and as large columns of baggage & troops were moving down what I suppose was the MONS - MAUBEUGE road I decided to follow them.

As the men were already tired after their exertions & countermarching on 23rd I ordered them to dismount their kits.

5

We then moved off to the MAUBEUGE road where the odd companies left me to rejoin their units, & after moving my men clear of the road I again tried to ascertain the whereabouts of the division.

I now met Capt Price Davies of the staff of   and ascertained that the 3rd division was on the left of the army moving towards BAVAI, & therefore decided to strike across country to try & join it.

Meanwhile the 1st line transport had unfortunately been swept down the MAUBEUGE road with the other masses of vehicles going in this direction, & was not recovered for several days.

Eventually we reached BLAIREGNIES and here I met Lt Col Maurice, G.S.O. 2 of 3rd division, who directed me to take up a rear guard position in this neighbourhood.

We were however, relieved by B/Genl Shaw's 9° brigade, & moved on reaching TAISNIERES at about 5 P.M., where a meal was obtained for all ranks.

We then moved to BAVAI & took up a position on its outskirts until about 5 P.M., where the remainder of 7th brigade appeared & we moved via ST WAAST to LE PLAT DE BOIS with outposts towards LA FLAMENGRIE.

Here some food was found dumped.

Touch was established with the division on our left & the night passed without incident.

25th Aug   Next day the battalion was rear guard to the 7th brigade.

6.

The outposts were withdrawn at 8AM & we fell back by stages to GOMMEGNIES, I think, without having seen the enemy.
From GOMMEGNIES we marched to LE QUESNOY.

Here we found the H.Q. of 11th Hussars & halted for a time occupying some of the fortifications.
B/Genl McCracken now ordered me to send a company along the railway towards POTELLE to help some howitzers said to be in difficulties, but luckily the order was cancelled & we moved off at about 3.30PM towards SCLESMES, being now some distance behind the brigade.

> At about this time some country people reported 600 German cavalry to be coming towards us.

Soon afterwards a Signaller cyclist came to me & said "I think you should see this message before I take it to the division."
The message was that two large columns of the enemy were close behind, & that one of two cavalry regiments, a mass of artillery & a large body of infantry was moving on LE QUESNOY.
This information was passed to the brigade, but we were ordered to continue our retirement.

> A message was also received from Lt Col Pitman 11th Hussars that he would hold on in LE QUESNOY as long as possible, but did not expect to be able to check the enemy for any length of time.

This we did in the usual fashion, companies relieving one another in favourable positions, and as we were not attacked & the men were becoming exhausted from moving across country, I sent my senior major, when we reached PONT À PIERRES, to request that we might be relieved.

7.

A message was returned that we should be relieved after passing through ROMERIES.

This place was entered at about 5.30 AM & when the battalion was in the centre of the village further progress was stopped by a mass of artillery which came from the direction of VERTAIN & trotted towards the X roads near the V of VERTIGNEUL.
My senior major having informed me that this was our direction we followed the artillery. Meanwhile the enemy had begun to shell ~~some~~ ROMERIES with shrapnel but most of them fell in the north end of the place.
We cleared the village at about 6 P.M. & on issuing found no infantry but a considerable body of our cavalry.
I moved the battalion under cover to the X roads about 400x east of the S of SOLESMES (second S) [?last S] having sent the senior major & adjutant to try & find the brigade.
They failed to do so & reported SOLESMES on fire.
Meanwhile the enemy's pursuit had ceased, & seeing B[riga]d[ier] Gen[era]l Briggs — cavalry brigade, on the high ground near the L of LE BEART I rode up & asked him if he could tell me anything about the division.

He confessed ignorance & said that he himself was going to take his brigade to LE CATEAU.
I asked if I could accompany him, &

a guide having been obtained from a neighbouring village we moved off at nightfall via AMERVAL the cavalry following.

At about 10 PM we reached the HALTE north of MONTAY coming along a road full of cavalry horses through which we had to force our way. I saw no outposts, but there was semaphore signalling going on as we neared MONTAY. After collecting my men at the HALTE I sent into the town to try & get information but without success.

I now came across Maj Bruce, commanding a battery of 3rd division, & he rode into LE CATEAU & getting into telephonic communication with H.Q. 2nd corps ascertained that we — the battery & battalion — were to move to REUMONT.

{and passing there were numerous bivouacs along the INCHY & REUMONT roads}

Accordingly we marched through LE CATEAU & after going some distance along the INCHY road

26th August — reached REUMONT at about 2 AM where I saw Genl Sir C Fergusson & Lt Col Romer his G.S.O.1.

Map 1/250,000

I was now directed to move to MAUROIS as escort to the supply column, as some enemy cavalry patrols were said to be about.

{When in LE CATEAU Lt Col Wanless & about a company of the S Lancashire Regt joined us for a short time but we lost them again in the town which was crowded with troops}

MAUROIS was reached at about 4 AM & the men went into billets & got a meal.

I waited about for some time expecting that the 5th division would move through MAUROIS, but as nothing happened lay down at 6 AM. At 7.30 AM I received a message from H.Q. 2nd corps that we were to parade at once & march to BERTRY.

9.

At BERTRY Major Cory of H.Q. 2nd Corps was sent to guide us to a locality south of CAUDRY which was to be held in case the Germans broke through, & the ~~divisional~~ corps escort ½ company of Highlanders was also placed at my disposal.

I placed the Highlanders near the railway bridge ½ a mile south of the A of AUDENCOURT & proceeded to entrench from the stud farm one mile north of MONTIGNY to the CAUDRY—CLARY road.

At about noon I was ordered to send half a company into CAUDRY & did so.

At about 3 P.M. Maj Genl Hamilton came up & asked whether I was the senior Lt Col in the brigade, as B Genl McCracken had been stunned by a shell.

I said I was, & he then told me that he wished to clear CAUDRY & would place my battalion, such other troops of 7th brigade – i.e. some companies of Wiltshires & Worcesters – as were not in the village, and also the Welsh Fusiliers & Middlesex (I think) at my disposal for this purpose, together with 2 batteries, that under Maj Bruce, & another. The Highland ½ company had meanwhile come under shell fire & withdrawn.

Maj Genl Hamilton then rode away & almost immediately I received a message that the division was to retire.

Maj Genl Hamilton returned soon afterwards & I told him of this & also pointed out

that the enemy's attack on LIGNY-EN-
CAMBRESIS seemed to be progressing.
He said, however that this did not matter
& told me to carry on.

Before any definite action could be taken
Lt Col F Maurice G.S.O. 2, woke up with
orders for the withdrawal of the division,
& very soon afterwards LIGNY was taken
& the enemy opened fire on us from it.

Maj Genl Hamilton then ordered me to
withdraw the troops of 7th Brigade from
CAUDRY and cover the retirement with
my battalion & the two batteries.

I accordingly sent orders for the evacuation
of CAUDRY placed my battalion in the
enclosures near the stud farm, & to the
south of it, & posted Bruce's battery behind
our right & the other behind our left.
The latter battery did not wait long &
the C.O. soon sent me word that he was
withdrawing.

At about 4.30PM, when CAUDRY had
almost been cleared, the bulk of the
artillery & infantry that had been defending
AUDINCOURT suddenly came streaming
down the hill to the railway, then taking
the road to MONTIGNY.

First came some guns & limbers at full
gallop, the guns, limbers etc covered with
infantrymen, then the infantry in complete
disorder.

We watched them pass us, & as soon as
they had cleared the slopes down to the railway
Maj Bruce opened fire on the hill crest

between AUDINCOURT and CAUDRY.
The Germans made no attempt to pursue & after waiting about 20 minutes since there was no sign either of more of our men or of any of the enemy coming from AUDINCOURT or CAUDRY I rode back & obtained Major Genl Hamilton's permission to retire.
We then marched via ELINCOURT and SERAIN to BEAUREVOIR, which the battalion reached at about midnight after forcing their way through masses of transport blocking the approaches.

27th August We paraded at 2.30AM. and the column marched, not in very good order, via ESTREES to BELLE ENGLISE. A good many men tried to fall out & pick up biscuits & meat left in the bivouacs we passed, as they had had nothing to eat since about 2 P.M. when some food reached us during the action at LE CATEAU.
We halted from about 9AM - 12 noon or 1PM near BELLE ENGLISE my battalion furnishing a few outposts.
The brigade then moved off, B Genl McCracken ordering me to undertake rearguard & to withdraw to the N of LE VERGUIER taking the road to VENDELLES, which was pointed out to me.
We fell back slowly without being molested picking up a company of Worcesters and five batteries of artillery, but could find no trace of the brigade, which had apparently changed its route on being shelled by the Germans

After passing through VENDELLES we met
an officer in a motor car, who said he had
been sent by H.Q. 4th division to ask for
assistance, as the division was hard
pressed. I agreed to move towards the division
& marched to, I think, SOYECOURT.
Here we halted at about 3.30 P.M. & I sent
an artillery officer to Genl Snow's H.Q.
to report my arrival & ascertain his wishes.

At about 4.30 P.M. the officer returned with
a written message from the G.S.O.I of the
division to the effect that we were to
remain at SOYECOURT until nightfall
when "your detachment will be broken
up & you are at liberty to rejoin your
division."
While I was wondering how best to act
Maj Paul Hamilton rode up & asked where
I had been & what I was doing.
I explained the situation & he said that
as all seemed quiet I had better "make
it nightfall & move to Vermand where I
should find the division."
We accordingly marched to Vermand
arriving at dusk & found great difficulty
in forcing our way through masses of
transport to a field where the 7th Brigade
had halted.
Here we had a meal & at 10.30 P.M. marched
28th August off again reaching HAM at daybreak, in
thick fog.
After a long halt we moved through HAM &

13.

bivouacked for 3 or 4 hours to the south west of it.

The brigade then marched off via GUISCARD to NOYON, & at about 5 P.M. we billeted in some villages east of the road & 2 miles from NOYON, very tired after our long marches.

29ᵗʰ August We rested until noon on 29ᵗʰ when the brigade took up a line of outposts in the big wood which extends N.E. of NOYON, the Irish Rifles being on the left & in touch with Genl Shaw's brigade on the GUISCARD - NOYON road.

The paths in the wood were narrow & overgrown, the wood very dense, & as night began to come on the wood became very dark.

I therefore rode to the Brigadier, who was in SALENCY, & suggested that if a further retirement were in contemplation it would be as well to withdraw from the wood while we could see our way.

He said, however, that we must remain in position & withdraw at 2 A.M.

I pointed out the great difficulty of doing so & asked him to send a staff officer into the wood to report on the situation. This he refused to do.

I then told one of my battalion interpreters, whom I had brought with me, to get two gardes-forestiers from the village & persuade them to come with us into the wood.

I took one man to my second in command

whom I put in charge of 2 companies & went to the remainder myself with the other man.

Connecting files were placed at 25ʸ interval between the groups & companies since it was so dark that one could not see one's hands even.

30th August — Having drawn in the groups we began to retire at 2 AM, the men moving in file & holding onto each other's clothing or rifles so as not to lose touch.

At grey dawn ~~through wood~~ we had cleared the wood & found ourselves, in a thick fog, in the valley of the OISE. Our guides however served us well and at about 6.30 AM we crossed the river at VARESNES, I think, just before the bridge was blown up, & here we found the rest of the brigade.

~~The brigade then marched to ATTICHY~~ ~~Here we found our train which waited for a few hours.~~

3○th August — The brigade marched through VILLERS COTTERETS ~~to bivouac~~ in a park near PISSELEUX or COYOLLES.

1st September — On ~~1st~~ we moved to ? arriving at dusk. An attack was apparently expected for in the afternoon the battalion was deployed for about an hour near a village where 2nd corps H.Q. were placed, & a position was also selected in the evening for occupation if required.

2nd September — We made a short march & halted at (?) VINCY.

3rd September — The brigade marched late in the day to a small village near BARCY arriving after nightfall.

Orders were then received that we were to find outposts, & to be in position by

3 A M or 4 A M from the x of something to the y of something else the Irish Rifles being N of BARCY.

It is not easy even in daylight to recognise localities so described, but at night & in an unknown country the difficulty is a good deal accentuated!

However, I sent officers out to reconnoitre routes, & the battalion reached approximately the positions allotted to it at the time it was required to do so.

4 September The battalion with the divisional cyclists formed the brigade rear guard & gradually fell back to MEAUX without getting into touch with the enemy.

We covered preparations for the destruction of the bridges which was accomplished at about 4 P.M. by the Engineers, & then marched to VAUCOURTOIS where we bivouacked.

5 September The battalion took up outposts at about 4 P.M., in touch with a company of Shropshire(?) L.I. on the MEAUX – COULOMMIERS road.

A few German cavalry were about.

At 10 P.M. we were ordered to withdraw & with the divisional cyclists form the rear guard. We were to march via CRECY-TIGEAUX & through the forest of CRECY.

The brigade went direct from CRECY through the forest so we lost touch for a time.

Moving via NEUFMOUTIERS & picking up about 150 stragglers of drafts recently come from England, we reached a farm about 1½ miles N of CHÂTRES at 8.30 A.M. – 9 A.M. Here we bivouacked in a field.

our train which we had not seen since ATTICHY was a mile away & we were therefore able to get the waterproof sheets from it & issue them to the men who were in need of something to cover them at night in bivouac.

6th September. On 6th the brigade marched at about 7 A.M. & we slowly retraced our steps through the forest of CRÉCY via MORTCERF & FARMOUTIERS, then through COULOMMIERS to billets at AULNOY(?) where we settled down at 11 P.M. ~~Here we were joined by a draft of our officer & 60 men.~~

7th September Next day we marched off at daybreak the 2nd R.I. Rifles being advanced guard to the brigade. No enemy was encountered until nightfall when the S Lancashire, who were on outpost duty, had some fighting in or near LA FERTE SOUS JOUARRE. The remainder of the brigade bivouacked in a field covered by sentries.

8th September Apparently a body of Germans was E or S.E. of LA FERTE over night & taking advantage of the darkness moved across our outpost front back over the MARNE.
As a result the S. Lancashire & also Genl Gough's cavalry brigade which was E or S.E of 3rd division had some fighting, & on the morning of 9th the 2nd R.I.R. were sent across the river to at LA FERTE to support the S Lancashire.
My orders were not to attack, but to come back over the MARNE when relieved by 5th division.
At about noon Count Gleichen's brigade appeared & we repassed the river.

17.

After moving in an easterly direction we bivouacked, I think, near BEZU(?)

9th September — This was a long day of halt & march & finally at nightfall we went into billets at ?

10th September — Another long day uneventful except that one continually passed German bivouacs covered with wine bottles, or houses whose gardens were also littered with bottles.
At nightfall we were billeted in a small village.

11th September — We marched at daybreak the 2nd R.I. Rifles & Cyclists forming divisional advanced guard.
At NEUILLY ST FRONT (I think) we came upon the 2nd division.
The 3rd division then crossed the OURCQ moving to GRAND ROZOY where we arrived at about noon & bivouacked in a field.
At 2 P.M. heavy rain came on & the brigade went into such cover, barns etc as the village afforded.
One company of R.I.R. was on outpost duty.

12th September — The weather cleared for a time & the brigade marched off.
In the afternoon rain began again & eventually, at about 9 P.M., we went into billets at CERSEUIL near BRAINE

13th September — On 13th the brigade moved off at daybreak through BRAINE and assembled in a field near LA SAULE SUDREE.
The enemy fired a few shells in this direction

but they fell short.

Towards evening the brigade moved back a little under cover & bivouacked.

14th September. During the night 13/14th September four sets of orders were received.

The first ordered the men of the brigade to be ready to march at 2.30 A.M. This was soon cancelled & the hour fixed at 5 A.M.; later this was changed to 7 A.M. or 8 A.M. Finally at about 4.30 A.M. the order came to move at 5 A.M.

Luckily the R.I.R reveille hour was left at 4 A.M. so the men had a meal before moving off.

In drizzling rain we moved towards CHASSEMY and then via AUDEBERT F.M.

Here I was ordered to take my battalion & the Wiltshire across the AISNE by the railway bridge near ECLUSE.

As we were advancing the LINCOLNSHIRE regt fell back over the river & the C.O. Lt Col Smith, who had been slightly wounded, told me he had been driven off the hills on the N bank, & that the R Fusiliers who were with him, had also retired.

I thereupon placed the Wilts behind the canal embankment, & reported to B/Genl McCracken.

He ordered me to advance & accordingly the Wiltshires first and then the R.I. Rifles moved under cover along the railway embankment & then over a bridge made of a barge & planks, the railway bridge over the AISNE having been broken.

The enemy shelled us during the movement

19.

As the men had to move in single file this took some time.

I had ordered the Wilts, as soon as they crossed the river, to occupy the height at the L of LA FOSSE MARGUEIL & this they did without much trouble. The Irish Rifles were to move to the left of the Wilts to the ground near M of MARGUEIL, but I kept one company in reserve near the D of PRECORD.

After we had crossed the river the Lincolns followed, & I placed them behind our left near the word ROUTE.

It must now have been about 3 P.M. or 4 P.M. Not long afterwards Maj Spedding commanding 2 R.I. Rifles asked for reinforcements & I sent him the company held in reserve.

The battalion had apparently tried to move over the crest of the hill but had been forced by artillery fire to fall back after losing a few men. Our artillery from near ST AUDEBERT F.M. now threw some shells onto the hill which fell among the Wilts.

This was reported to Brigade H.Q. near ST AUDEBERT, with which signal communication had been established, together with a report on the general situation.

As a result a company of Worcesters (?) was sent over the river, which I placed in a hollow road at the foot of the hill as reserve. With the exception of intermittent shelling nothing more happened before nightfall, except that the Lincolns rejoined their brigade. We also established signal

Ammunition was also brought by carriers in bandoliers across the river & sent up to the battalions as required

communication with some of our cavalry at LES GRUZONS.

During the night there were several bursts of fire from our men, but no reports reached me & I do not think any serious attack was made by the Germans.

15th September. At daybreak on 15th B/Genl McCracken came over the river, & I rejoined my battalion. On arrival on the hillcrest I found the officers & men of A & C companies standing about, & on asking what they were doing I was told that they thought the Germans had retired. I at once ordered two officer's patrols to be sent out to clear up the situation.

I then went a little north & found Major Spedding who pointed out the enemy's trenches in a hollow 700x from us & told me that he had sent D company to occupy the edge of a wood some 300x from the enemy.

See sketch map attached.

I agreed that this was sound but demurred in regard to the officer selected for this duty as I had no confidence in his judgment & feared he might make a rash attack.

Major Spedding however assured me that strict orders had been given to him not to proceed beyond the wood.

I then asked how long ago D company had been sent & he replied 20 minutes.

As the distance to the edge of the wood was not more than a quarter of a mile & as no firing had been heard, I concluded that they probably the Germans had retired, & ordered A company to move forward east of the wood

21.

in support of D company

I now saw what I took to be a few Germans running away, & as this seemed to show that their trenches were still held signalled to A company to halt.

No firing however took place, & I therefore sent my adjutant to the commander of A company (Capt Durrant) to tell him to advance but to proceed with the greatest possible caution.

Maj Spedding now joined A company, and with the M Gun section the company moved forward. Almost immediately it began to attack by rushes & was met by heavy rifle, machine- -gun & artillery fire. The movements of the other company were hidden by the wood.

About now the officers patrols returned & reported one officer wounded & the enemy in force.

As it was obvious that our partial attack could not succeed I sent my adjutant for B company, which was in reserve*, for I feared that the enemy could counter attack. He lost his way & could not find it, so I went & brought it forward myself & placed it in position to cover the retirement of the other two companies

Meanwhile D company had succeeded in rushing a trench & taking a few prisoners, but being met with heavy artillery fire & counterattacked was driven into the wood where A company & the machine guns had also been forced to take shelter.

These companies now streamed in disorder out of the wood and I rallied them 200x or 300x further back behind the crest. The Germans dropped several percussion shells among us as the men were rallying.

* at caves & hollows on sketch map

22.

This abortive attack cost us 9 or 10 officers & 150 other ranks killed & wounded.
I estimate that there was forced a regiment, a machine gun company, 2 field & one or more heavy batteries opposite the Wilts & R.I. Rifles

I understand that the O.C. B company who was wounded, subsequently stated that he was under the impression that he had been sent forward to attack the Germans.

I asked the O.C. A company, who was also wounded, when I met him at home, why he had attacked, & he said that he had a faint recollection of having been told to advance with caution, but seeing the other company attacking he did so too.

Having made a report to brigade H.Q. I rearranged my battalion as shown in the sketch map & the men threw up cover with their entrenching implements. In the wood roots prevented much progress, & outside it we were soon on solid rock. The reserve was in natural caves or hollows of which there were several near our line.
Signal communication was established by our signallers with brigade H.Q. at the foot of the hill 800' away.
My position was in a hollow near the machine guns.
The Germans shelled us a little with shrapnel and at about 10 P.M. there was an alarm of enemy attack & a good deal of firing
During the afternoon our patrols brought in

23.

some of the wounded who had been left between the German trenches & our own.
The Company Q.M.S.'s reported during the day that they had rations ready at the foot of the hill & a party was sent for them.
Subsequently a party was sent off each evening for rations at about 9 P.M. & returned with them at dawn when they were issued.

16th September — This was a rainy & foggy day.
The enemy's field artillery fired intermittently ours not at all.
Whenever the fog lifted we could see men in widely extended order, 30-40 paces apart being dribbled down the hill into the German trenches.
We opened fire when the Germans were coming down in what we thought too large numbers & caused some casualties but at considerable expenditure of ammunition as the ranges were from 1000x - 1500x & visibility was poor.
During the day I obtained the intrenching tools from our 1st line transport and the men improved their cover as far as they could.
~~In the evening we were informed that country people~~
Touch was obtained with the R. Fusiliers on our left, & some more of our wounded brought in by our patrols.
In the evening we were informed that country people had reported that the Germans intended to attack during the night.

17th September — As nothing had happened by midnight I sent my adjutant with one private to ascertain whether there were signs of movement in the German lines.

24.

He went to & actually fell into a German trench & found everyone asleep.
I thereupon reported this to Brigade H.Q.
During the night the Germans shelled VAILLY and the hill sides behind us with some heavy batteries probably near JERLAUX. The compass direction of the flash & estimated range 4500ˣ were reported to Brigade H.Q.
This shelling caused some casualties including Major Spedding, my senior major who was in ~~Vailly~~ VAILLY with the ration party & also to receive a draft of men said to be waiting there. This draft consisted of 1 officer & 6 men.
During the morning my patrols reported no sign of movement in the German trenches & I therefore sent my adjutant to make a reconnaissance.
He returned & said he could see no one & had stood in the open 300ˣ from the trench without being fired at
I accordingly ordered D company to occupy the edge of the wood & patrol from it.
The company commander took his company forward & then sent word that he would like me to come & see the situation as the German trench appeared to be full of men.
I went to the edge of the wood & after consulting with him ordered him to fall back as the company would have been much exposed & the roots of the trees made entrenching difficult.
No sooner had the order been given than the enemy who seems to have discovered our presence began to shell the wood heavily & we had some casualties as we fell back. Our guns sent a few shrapnell into the Germans & things then quieted down.

{ A company of Worcesters was sent to support me on this day & placed in the caves behind C company

25.

The night passed without incident, except the usual shelling, & was rainy.

18th September. Rain again fell, I think.

The German artillery became more active & we were obliged to keep under cover most of the day.

We lost a few men from artillery fire, & some of our patrols met German patrols in the wood.

On 17th or 18th I was directed to send in a return giving the name - rank - service etc of the senior of each rank in the battalion from Major to private.

This took time to obtain & so far as the privates were concerned was almost impossible to obtain accurately in the circumstances - viz rain - trenches - enemy's fire.

However, we were continually pressed to furnish the information until finally after having sent in two returns I ventured to suggest that the 3rd Echelon could produce them far more accurately than I could.

An artillery subaltern came to our lines & I pointed out the direction of the enemy's guns as estimated & showed him a fuze we had picked up sent at 1500 metres.

Another subaltern came up on 19th, I think, & these two were the only officers not belonging to my battalion, or attached to it, who visited our position.

Nothing unusual occurred during the night of 18th/19th.

19th September

Early on 19th the Germans began to shell our position with shrapnell & continued, with pauses to do so all morning.

In the afternoon the shelling was more vigorous the battery attacking us firing "progressively" at 1500 metres. the usual procedure being two salvos shot one on our trenches one over. Probably the fact that trees were 50ˣ – 60ˣ behind us made it difficult for them exactly to locate our position, but the fire was accurate some shells bursting on graze on our parapets. The casualties were nevertheless comparatively few.

Between 2 P.M. & 3 P.M. I was sent for to go to Brigade H.Q. & walked down the hill. The Germans were now occasionally sweeping the hill side with H.E. shell probably 5.9".

I returned at about 4 P.M. & got safely into the cave behind B companys line & was waiting at the mouth of the cave for the shelling to moderate to go to my H.Q. A H.E. shell now burst in a tree on B coys line which we had been unable to fell for want of tools & I and 2 other officers were wounded.

At 6 P.M. the enemy attacked bringing up machine guns, but was easily beaten off.

Our artillery gave us no support at all & I believe was still on the south bank of the Aisne

20ᵗʰ September. The Germans attacked again just after I had been carried down to VAILLY advancing through the wood.

A good many casualties were caused by their machine gun fire from the wood, but the company of Worcesters being brought up by Capt Goodman of R.I.R. against the enemy's right through the wood the Germans at once fell back.

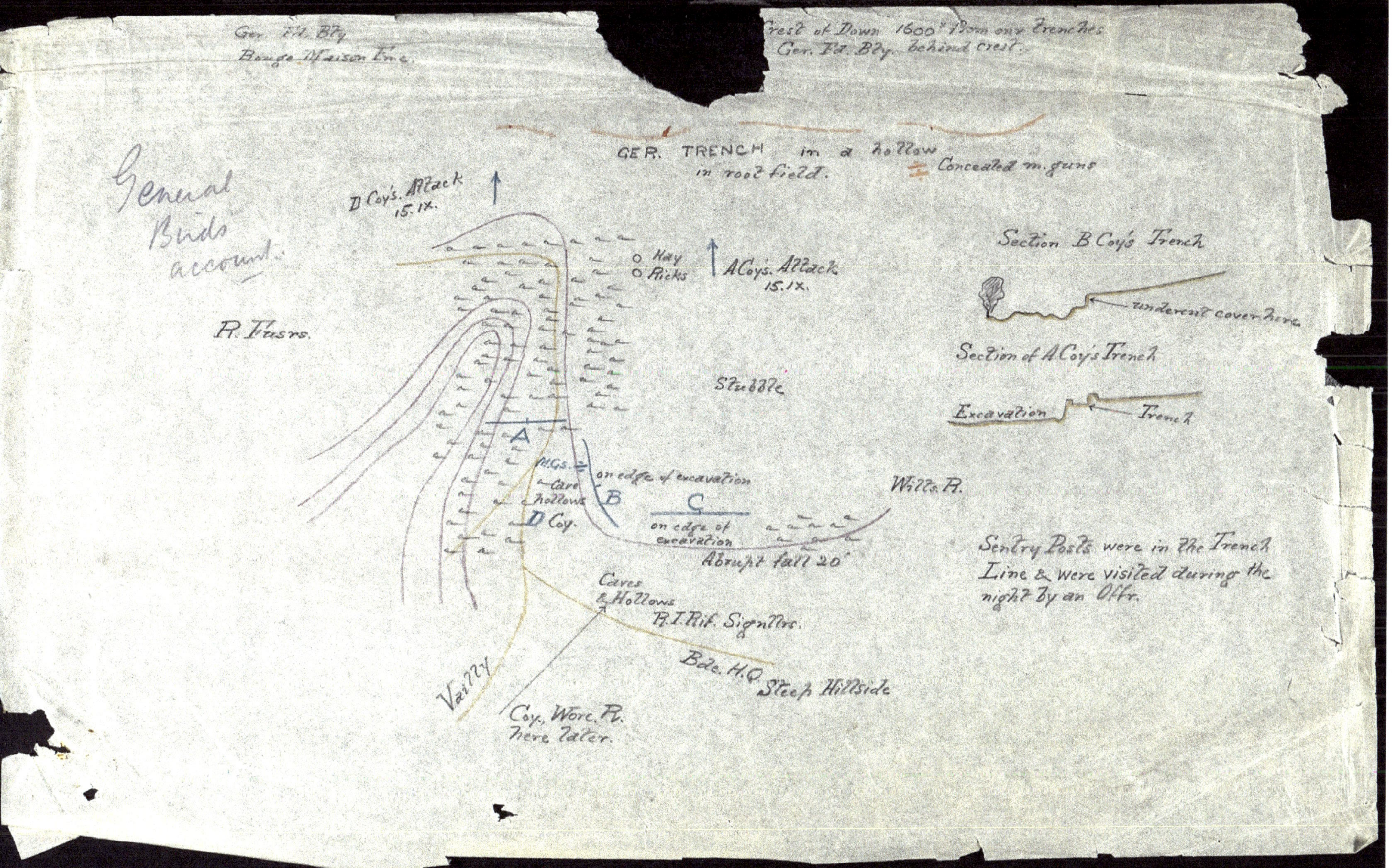

Ger. Fd. Bty
Bouge Maison Fme.
Crest of Down 1600' from our Trenches
Ger. Fd. Bty. behind crest.
General Birds account.
GER. TRENCH in a hollow in root field.
Concealed m. guns
D Coy's Attack 15.IX.
o Hay o Ricks
A Coy's Attack 15.IX.
Section B Coy's Trench
undercut cover here
Section of A Coy's Trench
Excavation
Trench
R. Fusrs.
Stubble
A
M.Gs.
on edge of excavation
Caves
Hollows
B
C
D Coy.
on edge of excavation
Wilts. R.
Abrupt fall 20'
Sentry Posts were in the Trench Line & were visited during the night by an Offr.
Caves & Hollows
R.I. Rif. Signllrs.
Bde. H.Q.
Steep Hillside
Valley
Coy. Worc. R. here later.

German Rifle fire
ROUGE MAISON F.M.

Crest of Down 150 x from our
trenches. Germans filled their front
trenches. Germans filled their front line & cont.
was concealed machine guns.

GERMAN TRENCH in a hollow
in root field

Section of B coy's trench
← cover underneath here
Section of A coy's trench
← trench
extension

Sentry posts were in the trench
line, & were visited during the
night by an officer.

Becq's attack
on 15th
O Haycocks ↑ A coy's attack on 15th
machine guns
B Company on edge of excavation
A Company
Cave & hollow D Company
Company on edge of an excavation
Almost falls for 20 ft.
Stubble
Wiltshire
Caves & hollows
R.I.R. Signallers
To Bgde H.Q.
Gully
Steep hill side
Company of Worcestershire
later
Royal Fusiliers

SUBJECT:- **Historical.**

REF: 318/2

The Officer i/c Historical Section,   Mustapha Pasha Barracks,
(Military Branch);   Alexandria, Egypt.
The War Office,   30th March, 1931.
London.

Sir,

        I recently received some old papers from my Mother's house and amongst them I came across the originals of the enclosed messages.

        They were in my pocket when I was wounded at Mons on the 24th August, 1914, and came back with me to England. I remember sealing them up and marking them to Records in the event of my death.

        From two of the messages you will see that the position allotted to the 7th Ifantry Brigade, (less 2nd Royal Irish Rifles) was somewhat different to the position shown on Map 7, Vol.1, Official History.

        I can vouch that the position given in Brigade Major. B.M. 70 dated 23.8.14 was the one actually taken up by 1st Wilts. I was Adjutant of the Battalion at the time.

        As the original messages can be of no great value to the Historical Section, I request permission to retain them and insert them in the Digest of Services of the 1st Bn. The Wiltshire Regiment.

        I have the honour to be,

        Sir,

        Your obedient servant,

V. T. Cowan.
Lieut-Colonel,
Commanding, 1st Bn. The Wiltshire Regiment.

O.C. 1/Wilts. Regt.

BM18.   22/8/14.

Please report whether your company has occupied HARMIGNIES AAA If Capt. Richards has not reported send an officer to ascertain

R. Hildyard, Capt.

True Copy

T.S. Cowan. Lt.Col.
Alexandria   Cmdg 1st Bn. The Wiltshire Regt.
29th March 1931.

O.C. 1/Wilts Regt.

Following message received from H.Q. 3rd
Division (begins) Troops will remain
generally in the position reached tonight
but certain alterations within the area
and readjustments of outpost line will
be made AAA These will be communicated
later

      Sd R. HILDYARD
       Bde. Maj.
       7th Inf. Bde.

CIPLY
22-8-14.

True Copy.

T. S. Cowan. Lt. Col.

Alexandria.
29th March 1921. Cmdg 1st Bn. The Wiltshire Regiment.

O.C. 1/Wilts. Regt.

The Germans are reported in strength at BRAY and PERONNES AAA It is possible that an attack may be delivered against our line which will run roughly from 11th Kilometre on GIVRY - PATURAGE road to SINENNES AAA

Your Company at HARMIGNIES in conjunction one company R.I.R. at NOUVELLES which has been told to get in touch with you, will take up a position covering HARVENG AAA Tools should be taken to entrench position AAA

The company should be in position at 4.30 a.m. AAA

The remainder of the Battalion at CIPLY must stand to arms at 4.30 a.m. ready to move off on receipt of orders wagons packed and horses hooked in AAA

An officer to report to Bde. Headquarters at 4.30 a.m.

     R. Hildyard,
      Bde. Major,
       7th Inf. Bde.

True Copy.
T. T. Cowan. Lt. Col.
Cmdg. 1st Bn. The Wiltshire Regiment

Alexandria
29th March 1931.

O.C. 1/Wilts. Regt.

    Please report if your Battalion is in possession of travelling kitchen and say if horses and harness of kitchens are supplied.

    Very Urgent.

                          Bde. Major,
                          7th Inf. Bde.

                                    A.H.
                                  23-8-14.

2nd ROYAL IRISH RIFLES
AND 1st WILTS.

BM.67.   23rd.

7th Infy. Bde. is to entrench a position from point 76 NORTH of NOUVELLES to I of BELIAN and thence to railway at a point just EAST of 3rd KILOMETRE on the MONS FRAMERIES ROAD AAA   COL. BIRD will be in charge of the right sector and will have 1st WILTS REGT under your command AAA   Right sector point 76 NORTH of NOUVELLES to RIVER RAU both inclusive AAA   You are to entrench your sector as fast as you can AAA   You can engage as much civilian labour as required 5 francs a day of 10 hours work AAA   Am endeavouring to obtain civil labour as well AAA   The road should be barricaded to prevent egress from MONS and should if possible be swept by fire from your positions AAA   Addressed O.C. IRISH RIFLES repeated 1st WILTS.

R. Hildyard Capt.

7th BDE.
CHATEAU CIPLY
12.40 p.m.

True Copy.

T. S. Cowan. Lt. Col.
Cmdg 1st Bn. The Wiltshire Regt.

Alexandria
29th March 1921.

O.C. Wilts.

BM 70.

R.I.R. are being detached for the present AAA

The position is therefore divided as follows pending arrival of R.I.R. when the first order will hold good AAA

1st Wiltshire Regt. point 76 just North of NOUVELLES to the I in BULIAN AAA

3rd Worcesters thence to Railway running from Railway works to CIPLY AAA

2nd South Lancashire thence to railway opposite 3rd Kilometre.

Acknowledge.

        R. Hildyard Capt.
         Capt.
        Bde. Major,
        7th Inf. Bde.

23.8.14.   True Copy

Alexandria
29th March 1931. Cmdg. 1st Bn The Wiltshire Regt.

1/Wilts.

Issue to all men additional ammunition AAA Go on strengthening trenches during the night AAA Be prepared for attack by day and night AAA Bde. Headquarters cross roads north of C of CIPLY AAA State anything we can do for you AAA Send all empty carts to Brigade Headquarters

R. Hildyard Capt.

7th Inf. Bde.
7.40 p.m.

True Copy.
T. A. Cowan Lt. Col.
Cmdg 1st Bn. The Wiltshire Regt.
Alexandria
29th March 1931.

To H.Q. 1/Wilts.

23.8.14.

1. Capt. Cordon gave me an order from Brigade H.Q. 7th Inf. Bde. to send out scouts to find Ammunition Column 42nd Brigade and when found to order them to report as soon as possible to 7th Inf. Bde. H.Q.

2. An Ammunition Column passed H.Q. 1/Wilts. at 5 p.m. today making for NOUVELLES. No. of Bde. not known.

3. Cpl. Preece is bearer of this message and has two scouts with him.
Please give them orders.

                T.H. WAND-TETLEY, Lt.
                      1 Wilts. Rgt.

Despatched 8.45 p.m.

O.C. Wilts.

BM73   24th.

Have   not   yet   been   able
to   collect ROYAL   IRISH   RIFLES
AAA   State   how   many   men
you   require on   your   right
and   left   respectively

        7th Bde.
        FORKED ROADS.
        N of C in CIPLY 1.29

True Copy.
J. S. Cowan. Lt.Col.
Alexandria
29th March 1921.   Cmdg 1st Bn The Wiltshire Regt.

7th Brigade.
3rd Division.

2nd BATTALION

ROYAL IRISH RIFLES.

SEPTEMBER 1 9 1 4

8am 1-9-14	COYOLLES	Marched about 8am via VAUCIENNES - LEVIGNEN to VILLERS - ST GENEST & bivouac.
2-9-14	VILLERS	Marched in early morning via BOUILLANCY - MARCILLY - BARCY to PRINGY & bivouac.
2-9-14	PRINGY	
8am 3-9-14	PRINGY	Marched 3am to LA MARCHE & bivouac.
10am 3-9-14	LA MARCHE & ST SOUPPLETS	Enemy's cavalry & infantry reported 1 mile North of rear guard position. Moved off about 10am to rearline via PENCHARD - MEAUX - BOUTIGNY to SANCY & bivouac.
6pm 4-9-14	SANCY	Moved about 6pm & took up outpost position covering VAUCOURTOIS. Withdrew during the

Covering 79 / 3208

INTELLIGENCE SUMMARY.

(Erase heading not required.)

Hour, Date, Place	Summary of Events and Information	Remarks and references to Appendices
5-9-14 CHATRES	Night — resumed march via CRECY - OBELISQUE - NEUFMOUTIERS to near CHATRES, & bivouac.	
5-9-14 CHATRES	In bivouac N. of CHATRES. 1st Reinforcement arrived.	
6-IX-14 CHATRES	Marched about 8 am via NEUFMOUTIERS - OBELISQUE to FAREMOUTIERS & bivouac. Halted a long time in the FORET DE CRECY.	
7-IX-14 FAREMOUTIER	Marched in morning via COULOMMIERS to LES PETITS AULNOIS & partly billetted — partly bivouac. 2nd Reinforcement arrived under Lt. Mayersen — 3/R.I. Rifles	
7-IX-14 LES PETITS AULNOIS		
8-IX-14 BUSSIERES	Marched in morning via REBAIS to BUSSIERES. Two companies, C.D. & Belfast, some wounded Germans picked up.	
9-IX-14 BUSSIERES	Marched in aming D by rear guard 173rd. Wanted NANTEUIL - CROUTTES to BEZU & bivouac. Received information the Germans were retiring across our front.	
10-IX-14 BEZU	Marched in morning via CHEZY to MONTMARROY & billetted.	
11-IX-14 GRAND ROZOY	Marched in morning to GRAND-ROZOY via DAMMARD - NEUILLY - OULCHY LA VILLE & bivouac. Two coy's on outpost. Patro advanced front to R. ?	

INTELLIGENCE SUMMARY.

(Erase heading not required.)

Hour, Date, Place	Summary of Events and Information	Remarks and references to Appendices
12-IX-14 GRAND ROZOY	Marched in Brigade via LES CROUTES - MAAST to CERSEUIL & partly billetted & partly slept in a cave. Weather very wet.	
13-IX-14 CERSEUIL 13-IX-14 BRAINE	Marched following morning to BRAINE & billetted Reverie in BRAINE & bivouaced there at night.	
14-IX-14 BRAINE	Marched about 6am via BRENELLE & halted some time near point 164. Moved via CHASSEMY to BOIS MORIN. Turned off by country road & moved towards railway bridge over AISNE. (Road AISNE by infantry foot-bridge built alongside railway bridge which had been blown up. As soon as head of column approached bridge enemy commenced to open fire with their guns - a few casualties. D Company said "Forty" Coys. & ground at LA FOSSE MARGNET on left of WILTS Regt. A Coy followed & took up position further back on left. ½ D Coy moved forward & commenced entrenching but had Hosene back owing to very fired on by our own artillery. Capt. Scooby A Coy	Wounded Capt. Gifford " Lt. Cowley

INTELLIGENCE SUMMARY.

(Erase heading not required.)

Hour, Date, Place	Summary of Events and Information	Remarks and references to Appendices
15-IX-14 VALLEY OF AISNE	was slightly wounded today & a few other casualties. Outburst of rifle fire during the night but nothing seen.	
	Officers patrol from D Coy under Lt Davis was ordered forward to ascertain whereabouts of enemy. Came under heavy fire, Lt Davis & one man wounded, 1 man killed, two men caught. A & C Coys ordered forward to attack, came under heavy fire, artillery, machine guns & rifle & were compelled to fall back, a good many casualties. The following officers were killed 2/Lt Sessions, 2/Lt Mogannam (?) (3/A.t.Rifles). Following wounded Captains Bowen, Colthurst, Durant, 2/Lts Peebles, Yarwell. Battn remained in position on the hill D Company reinforcing A Company, B Company moved up too, the left flank. Position was shelled throughout the day, some casualties.	
5pm 15-IX-14 VALLEY of AISNE	Enemy attacked about 5pm, attack ceased about 9.15pm.	

INTELLIGENCE SUMMARY.

(Erase heading not required.)

Instructions regarding War Diaries and Intelligence Summaries are contained in F.S. Regs., Part II. and the Staff Manual respectively. Title pages will be prepared in manuscript.

Hour, Date, Place	Summary of Events and Information	Remarks and references to Appendices
16-IX-14 VALLEY of AISNE	Spent day entrenching. Shelled intermittently all day.	
17-IX-14 " "	C Company sent forward to entrench an advanced position but were driven back by shell fire. Position shelled on + off all day. Some casualties.	
18-IX-14 " "	Position shelled intermittently. Infant regiment frozen? Wiltshire regt that the Germans had broken through on their right.	
19-IX-14 " "	Very heavy or continuous bombardment which lasted till dark. Following officers wounded Lt. Col. Bond D.S.O., Capt. Becher, Lt. + Adjt. Dillon Lt. Cowley. A good many casualties. A fairly severe attack took place about 6.30pm which lasted till about 8pm. Two platoons of 7th Hances Fusiliers Regt came up in support.	
20-IX-14 " "	Slight bombardment after daybreak. About 10 am a severe attack took place supported by artillery. This attack lasted a little over two hours. One Company S. Lancs Regt came up to support. Wounded Capt. Bedlem.	

INTELLIGENCE SUMMARY.

(Erase heading not required.)

Instructions regarding War Diaries and Intelligence Summaries are contained in F.S. Regs., Part II. and the Staff Manual respectively. Title pages will be prepared in manuscript.

Hour, Date, Place	Summary of Events and Information	Remarks and references to Appendices
20-IX-14 VALLEY of AISNE	A report was received from Wiltshire Regt that the Germans had broken through on their right. 2nd Reinforcements joined exige 2nd Battalion. Quiet during the day. A severe attack took place about dusk supported by artillery & machine guns, attack lasted about 2 hours. Intermittent firing all night. About 1am 22-IX-14 received information that the Leicestershire Regt were to relieve the Battn on the hill. Relief completed by 3am & the Battn marched down to VALLEY. The following casualties occurred during the period 14-IX-14 to 21-IX-14 VALLEY of AISNE. **Killed** 2/Lt Swaine 2/Lt Moggridge (3 A.I. Rifles) Other Ranks 39 (as far as can be estimated) Died of wounds. 5	
21-IX-14 " "		

INTELLIGENCE SUMMARY.

(Erase heading not required.)

Hour, Date, Place	Summary of Events and Information	Remarks and references to Appendices
VALLEY of AISNE	Wounded Lt-Col W. D. Bird D.S.O. Capt. F. C. Bowen — to Others " T. L. B. Soutry " A. L. Giffard " A. N. Durant " C. M. L. Becher (twice) Lieut A. E. Beebles " V. L. S. Cowley (twice) " R. S. Vansell " C. R. B. Dawes " G. S. Norman Lt-a-Adj S.S. Dillon Other ranks 226 Missing Major C. R. Spedding D.S.O.	

INTELLIGENCE SUMMARY.

(Brass heading not required.)

Instructions regarding War Diaries and Intelligence Summaries are contained in F. S. Regs., Part II. and the Staff Manual respectively. Title pages will be prepared in manuscript.

Hour, Date, Place	Summary of Events and Information	Remarks and references to Appendices
VALLEY of AISNE	The following officers marched down the hill with the Battn. on relief by the Leics. Yeshire Regt- Major R. A. C. Daunt. D.S.O. (Commanding acting adjutant) Lt A. B. Hutchinson A Coy. Lt E. M. Thomas. B Coy Capt C. L. Master " H. A. Kennedy (Reserve of Officers) 2/Lt M. L. Godsoe. C Coy Capt- H. R. Goodman Lt- G. Lowry 6/K.R. Rifles D Coy Lt- A. N. Whitfield	

INTELLIGENCE SUMMARY.

(Erase heading not required.)

Hour, Date, Place	Summary of Events and Information	Remarks and references to Appendices
VALLEY of AISNE	Attached Capt: S.E. Lewis M.B.M.C. Sergt: L. Bertrand 39th Regt - Interpreter.	
3am 22-IX-14	Marched to VAILLY crossed AISNE and to AUGY & took up billets, 7.30am.	
22-IX-14 AUGY	Billets.	
23-IX-14 "	Billets.	
24-IX-14 "	Billets. Two companies under Capt. Grochewan moved out at 1pm to entrench a position W. of BRAINE.	
25-IX-14 "	Billets.	
7.30am 26-IX-14 "	Two companies under Capt. Martin to BRAINE - DHUIZEL road to dig trenches.	
11.am 26-IX-14 "	Received orders to proceed to CHASSEMY and relieve S. Lancashire Regt. on outposts.	

INTELLIGENCE SUMMARY.

(Erase heading not required.)

Instructions regarding War Diaries and Intelligence Summaries are contained in F.S. Regs, Part II. and the Staff Manual respectively. Title pages will be prepared in manuscript.

Hour, Date, Place	Summary of Events and Information	Remarks and references to Appendices
3 pm 26-IX-14 AUGY	Marched at 3pm and relieved S. Lancashire Regt. at CHASSEMY, taking up the position at dusk. A, B, D, Coys on outpost, C Company in reserve.	
4 am 27-IX-14 CHASSEMY	Received a report enemy advancing from 13th Inf. Bde that the enemy were crossing CONDÉ Bridge in large numbers. Marched all covering troops forward unsupported but quiet in the outpost line. A few of the enemy's shells over the village during the day.	
28-IX-14 CHASSEMY	All quiet in outpost line. Relieved by Wiltshire Regt in the afternoon. Wiltshire Regt. marched in by daylight and the enemy sent a few shells.	
9.30pm 28-IX-14 BRAINE	Reached BRAINE about 9.30 pm and took over Wiltshire's billets. Billets dirty.	
29-IX-14 BRAINE	In billets.	
30-IX-14 BRAINE	In billets. Received orders to march to COURVELLES. C Company in advance to clean up the village.	
2pm 30-IX-14	Marched to COURVELLES and went into billets.	
1-IX-14 COURVELLES	In billets. Two companies under Capt. Goodwin	

COPY OF LETTER ADDRESSED TO WING COMMANDER

S L E S S O R.

I have for some time been intending to write to you about he following statement made on page 690 of the Journal of the Royal United Service Institution of November, 1934.

"G.914. Aeroplane report timed 8.45AM and dropped with 3rd "divisions states considerable force of all arms collecting "behind woods......"

"The originators of this report can only have been Captain "Dawes and Lieut Crosbie of No 2 Squadron......"

On the 9th September, 1914, the battalion that I was then commanding, the 2nd Battalion Royal Irish Rifles, was waiting on the road leading northward to Nanteuil sur Marne when a single airman landed in a stubble field close to us. He walked up to me, asked where the headquarters of the 3rd Division was and whether he could borrow a horse in order to make a personal report to it. He told me that the Germans had a considerable force of infantry with guns on the hills north of the Marne, that the infantry were well hidden behind small woods, and that the Germans were preparing a surprise for us. We lent him the horse, and left a groom to wait for it who later brought the horse back to the battalion.

17.2.35.

7th Brigade.
3rd Division.

2nd BATTALION

ROYAL IRISH RIFLES.

OCTOBER 1 9 1 4

WAR DIARY
INTELLIGENCE SUMMARY.
(Erase heading not required.)

Army Form C. 2118.

Hour, Date, Place	Summary of Events and Information	Remarks and references to Appendices
1-X-14 COURCELLES	To BRAINE - DHUIZEL Road to dig trenches. Received orders to march to GRAND ROZOY.	
9.15pm 1-X-14	Marched at 9.15pm rejoining 7th Infy Bde at starting point near junction ½ mile N.W. of CERSEUIL at 10.15pm. Marched to GRAND ROZOY and went into billets about 4.30am. Batln finding two posts on roads today W.T.S.	
2-X-14 GRAND ROZOY	[In billets] Marched at 8.30pm via [ST REMY] BILLY s/OURCQ, [CHOUY] to NOROY and went into billets about 1.30am. D Cy finding 6 posts of 1 N.C.O. & 6 men each on roads leading into the village.	
1.30am 3-X-14 NOROY		
3-X-14 NOROY	[In billets] Marched at 7.40pm via TROESNES, LA FERTÉ MILON, COYOLLES to VAUMOISE & went into billets about 3am.	
3am 4-X-14 VAUMOISE		
4-X-14 VAUMOISE	In billets.	

WAR DIARY
or
INTELLIGENCE SUMMARY.
(Erase heading not required.)

Army Form C. 2118.

Hour, Date, Place	Summary of Events and Information	Remarks and references to Appendices
4th Oct. VAUMOISE	Arrived early morning & went into billets. Left VAUMOISE 7pm & marched via CREPY, BETHISY to VERBERIE & went into billets.	
5th Oct. VERBERIE	In billets. Received orders to entrain at Ry station of LONGUEIL STE MARIE at midnight. Left VERBERIE & crossed the OISE by the bridge of boats at PORT SALOT. Battn: entrained by 2 am.	
6th Oct.	In train. Arrived at NOYELLES about 4.30 pm and eventually received orders over the station telephone from ABBEVILLE to detrain and find billets for the night. Billeted the Battn: at NOYELLES.	
6th Oct. NOYELLES		
7th Oct. NOYELLES	In billets at NOYELLES. Received orders to march to LE PLESSIEL. Marched at 11.30 am via SAILLY, LE TITRE, HAUTVILLERS to LE PLESSIEL and went into billets. The Battn: finding posts round the village.	
8th Oct. LE PLESSIEL	In billets at LE PLESSIEL	

WAR DIARY or INTELLIGENCE SUMMARY.

Army Form C. 2118.

Hour, Date, Place	Summary of Events and Information	Remarks and references to Appendices
9th Oct: REGNAUVILLE 4.30 pm	Marched to REGNAUVILLE & went into billets. Marched at 4.30 pm to HESDIN where the Batt:n was moved by motor transport to FLORINGHEM. This move was carried out by the French & then afterwards tho' a considerable lack of method - a good deal of confusion was caused. Batt:n → Brigade getting mixed up. But eventually the Batt:n got settled out at FLORINGHEM & held an outpost line from the river CLARENCE on the east. rank of FLORINGHEM, though point 157 to the PERNES–SAINS road on the west.	
10th Oct: FLORINGHEM	On outpost round FLORINGHEM. The following officers joined this day. Capt:n Owen, Reynolds, Davies (3rd Bn), Smyth (6th Bn:) Lts Henn Brown, Lt G. Fitzgerald and Ranville (Kens to regt:) stated → 2/Lt Jones from hospital. rejoined by Manceston luk left in the afternoon and went into billets at PERNES	
11th Oct: PERNES HINGES.	Marched about 9 am via FLORINGHEM, AUCHEL, LOZIN=GHEM, ALLOUAGNE, GONNEHEM to HINGES and went into billets. Brigade very late getting into billets.	

Army Form C. 2118.

WAR DIARY
or
INTELLIGENCE SUMMARY.
(Erase heading not required.)

Hour, Date, Place	Summary of Events and Information	Remarks and references to Appendices
12th Oct: HINGES LACOUTURE.	Marched from HINGES. 2nd Lancashire Regt and two Coys 2/K.R.Rifles advance guard, two Coys 2/K.R.Rifles main body. Came up with enemy at LACOUTURE which was under shell fire. 2nd Lancs. crossed river LOISNET, found bridge head N. of stream. 2/K.R.Rifles reinforced 2nd Lancs one company at a time. A few casualties. Capt. Master killed. This portion was held during the night. During the night orders were received that the advance was to be continued next morning in conjunction with 8th Bde. to the line CROIX BARBEE to farm house N. of point S. in ST VAAST, the dividing line between brigades to be the LACOUTURE – CROIX BARBEE road. 2/K.R.Rifles on left of 7th & 8th Bde.	Casualties: Major Conducted by Major R.O.B. Lonel [?] Newille Maj R.I.R. Killed: Major Pownby 2/Bny R. Rifles.
13th Oct: LACOUTURE	Advance continued. Owing to the ruins & dikes it took some time to get the two Battns. out of the position at LACOUTURE as only one company could be got out at a time. The 8th Bde. got a little ahead but was soon caught up. The advance was continued and was carried to positn. of the Middlesex Regt. and staff of CROIX BARBEE, some of the Middlesex Regt. and C. Company 2/K.R.Rifles occupying the houses near cross roads at E. of CROIX BARBEE. The enemy were holding the	

WAR DIARY or INTELLIGENCE SUMMARY.

Army Form C. 2118.

(Erase heading not required.)

Hour, Date, Place	Summary of Events and Information	Remarks and references to Appendices
4 Oct: near CROIX BARBEE	village & the woods S. of it and some of their trawles ran in front of the village N. of the LACOUTURE road. Their artillery behind the village. During the afternoon an artillery officer brought information of an artillery gun going to shell CROIX BARBEE and is consequence reported our line. The withdrawn from close proximity to the village. A line was taken up from the group of houses midway between CROIX BARBEE & LACOUTURE. Middlesex Regt on our left & Lanc: on our right; then Coys in front line one in reserve. Capt Goodwin, Capt Smyth, 2/Lt Fitzgerald (Leins. to Regt.) attacked & two & then were wounded during the morning. Our artillery shelled CROIX BARBEE. Gun an artillery few of the enemy commenced to advance before dark. A few of the enemy connected to advance down the the LACOUTURE road but were soon driven back. Occupied the same position during the night. Occupied the same position. This day mostly taken up by our artillery shelling CROIX BARBEE & houses to the woods in vicinity. Occupied same position at night.	Thoms. Way Lt/Col consulted by Major R.C.B. Bond Little Major Copy of W/D 2 Bags of Bn/s

WAR DIARY or INTELLIGENCE SUMMARY

Army Form C. 2118.

Hour, Date, Place	Summary of Events and Information	Remarks and references to Appendices
14th Oct. near CROIX BARBEE	Moved forward in morning + took up old position just short of CROIX BARBEE. Lt Whitfield killed and Lt Heron wounded. Occupied same position at night. Soon after dark heavy firing broke out on the right and extended along the whole front, but the firing having lasted for 2 or 3 hours. Subsequent by ascertained this originated from a French night attack on VERMELLES.	Casualties: Lt Whitfield killed in action. Lt Heron —
15th Oct. near CROIX BARBEE	Occupied same position in morning. About 1.30pm received orders to advance was 6th continued at 2pm. Advance reached to a little past CROIX BARBEE + came under a continuous advance of front rifle + artillery fire but few casualties. Held line during the night from a point on the road a little S.W. of cross roads at ROUGE CROIX to the parallel roads leading into the NEUVE CHAPELLE — ESTAIRES road, 8th Btn on left, 5th Lancashires Regt on right.	Casualties by sniper R.O.B. Jones (signaller)
16th Oct. near ROUGE CROIX	Resumed advance next morning, covering by 8th Btn on left + finishing on S. Lanc on right. Halted some time on NEUVE CHAPELLE — FLEURBAIX road. Resumed advance in a slightly changed direction, the finishing line between 7th + 8th Btns being the road junction S.E. of the X of ROUGE CROIX to the N. corner of the BOIS DE BIEZ	

INTELLIGENCE SUMMARY.
WAR DIARY or INTELLIGENCE SUMMARY.
(Erase heading not required.)

Army Form C. 2118.

Hour, Date, Place	Summary of Events and Information	Remarks and references to Appendices
L'AVENTURE	Came under some shell fire near the BOIS DE BIEZ. No casualties. Held the line at night running N.E. from the BOIS DE BIEZ, 8th Bn. (Nicholls Rgt) on left, S. LANCS on right.	
17th Oct: BOIS DE BIEZ	Resumed advance. Right proved at Ht POMMEREAU, 8th Bn. on left, Wiltshire Rgt, vice S. Lancs, relieved, on right. Halted here some time & reconnoitred villages of L'AVENTURE. From L'AVENTURE Germans could be seen moving towards LA BASSÉE along the road from FOURNES, also a good deal of motor transport. Received message the 8th Bn. were going to attack HEAL HERLIES, advanced with 8th Bn., 3 coys in front line, 1 coy in reserve. Reserve coy left at L'AVENTURE, other three coys drawn off in the attack on HERLIES but were eventually recalled and the line straightened out in conjunction with the 8th Bn. Held line at night over LAUNOY, Wilts on right, 8th Bn. a little thrown back on left. A few casualties. About midnight received message the Batt: was to be relieved.	

WAR DIARY
INTELLIGENCE SUMMARY.
Army Form C. 2118.

Hour, Date, Place	Summary of Events and Information	Remarks and references to Appendices
18th Oct: L'AVENTURE	Batt: relieved by K.O.Y.L.I. about 5am and marched back Billets at PONT LOGY. About 3pm received orders to move: was en route from 6 to the BOIS DE BIEZ + later received orders to proceed to the BOIS DE BIEZ. Moved about 7 pm and occupied outpost line in front of the BOIS DE BIEZ. Held same position at night. Manchester Regt. on right.	Compiled by Major R.A.C. Daunt Major. [signature] Lieut & Adjt.
19th Oct: BOIS DE BIEZ	Held same position till about midday when orders were received from the Battn. to go into billets about the BOIS DE BIEZ in conjunction with the Manchester Regt. During the night orders were received for the Batt: to relieve the K.O.Y.L.I. at L'AVENTURE.	
20th Oct: BOIS DE BIEZ / L'AVENTURE	Marched about 4am to L'AVENTURE and relieved the K.O.Y.L.I. Taking up the former position near LANNOY. Wiltshire Regt. on right, Lincolns on left a little thrown back. A considerable amount of shelling during the day but no casualties. During the night orders were received to fall back on a partially prepared position along the road running through the second A of HALPEGARBE being "C" Company, "C", to hold the Bridge.	

WAR DIARY
INTELLIGENCE SUMMARY.
(Erase heading not required.)

Army Form C. 2118.

Compiled by Major R.O.C. Downs
Major,
Commd 3rd Royal Fus. Rgt.

Hour, Date, Place	Summary of Events and Information	Remarks and references to Appendices
Oct 21st L'AVENTURE	Marched about 1am to new position near HALPEGARBE & proceeded to entrench, a small portion of the line having been dug by the R.E. Three Coys in firing line, "D" Coy under Lt Symons being placed in reserve. Under a certain amount of shell fire all day which came from the right, enfilading the position, but no casualties. During the afternoon O.C. D Coy reported the enemy this morning across the front in a mass they divided. A section advanced & sniping during the day from the rear, apparently from the woods near to of the village. Orders were received & fell back on a prepared position at NEUVE CHAPELLE this movement to commence from the flanks of the Btn & to take place at midnight. The Batt. being on the left of the 13th Assembled at HALPEGARBE and moved off soon after midnight.	Account Attd R. I. Affairs
22nd Oct NEUVE CHAPELLE	Arrived at NEUVE CHAPELLE & took up new position. Three coys in trenches, one coy in reserve billetted in the School. About 6am moved Bn: headquarters & reserve company to Chateau, near road fork at N. end of village, as being more central & communication with trenches easier. Most of the day spent in digging reserve & communication	

INTELLIGENCE SUMMARY
or
WAR DIARY

Army Form C. 2118.

Instructions regarding War Diaries and Intelligence Summaries are contained in F.S. Regs., Part II. and the Staff Manual respectively. Title pages will be prepared in manuscript.

Hour, Date, Place	Summary of Events and Information	Remarks and references to Appendices
23rd Oct.	trenches. A certain amount of rifle fire from about foot of the enemy. The facilis had some disadvantages. A road on the left flank of the Batts: led towards the enemy with several houses along it which had not been destroyed. The 8th Btn on the left were echeloned back a considerable distance which was another disadvantage. This road above mentioned was entangled in the machine guns situated so as to command as long a stretch of the road as possible. They were however fired into clearing the night by the 8th Bt in rear. Patrols staying were fired into by other Battns: & some men killed. Later during the night there was some heavy firing along the line but the enemy was apparently not in any force. A few casualties.	Major R.O.C. Ward. Compiled by Major R.O.C. Ward.
Held same position with little change in the situation. Enemy attacked at night but repulsed. 24th 25th Oct:— NEUVE CHAPELLE	Enemy's fire became heavier towards evening. Gradually. Persistent shelling of the Field guns in the centre of the front line of trenches broke up the guns went out of action. The field guns in the trenches on the left remained in action. The enemy commenced a severe bombardment of NEUVE CHAPELLE from the heavy guns at LA BASSEE and from a heavy gun to our left front. The shells from LA BASSEE coming in series of four. A certain amount of shrapnel was fired but chiefly high explosive. Soon after dark a determined attack was made by the enemy in considerable	

INTELLIGENCE SUMMARY
WAR DIARY
or
INTELLIGENCE SUMMARY.
(Erase heading not required.)

Army Form C. 2118.

Instructions regarding War Diaries and Intelligence Summaries are contained in F.S. Regs., Part II. and the Staff Manual respectively. Title pages will be prepared in manuscript.

Hour, Date, Place	Summary of Events and Information	Remarks and references to Appendices
25th 16 Oct: NEUVE CHAPELLE 26	strength but was repulsed with heavy casualties judging by the noise made by German wounded lying in front of the trenches. Some prisoners wounded & unwounded were taken. Own casualties were not heavy. On morning 16th attack of the previous night the enemy succeeded in establishing themselves in the house was the left flank of the trenches and in the machinery used to the end trench on the left. They succeeded in capturing the field gun there but only fired one round out of it & this own turned it. With the remains of B Coy, in reserve (the remainder having replaced casualties in the firing line) and a platoon of the Lincolns Regt. the enemy were eventually driven out. but the trench could not be re-occupied as our own artillery were shelling it & the ground is very flat. To date this day, our artillery shelled the trenches held by the Batta: causing several casualties sent it was some time before they could be stopped as the telephone line was cut by shell fire and orderlies took a long time getting back. The enemy's bombardment this day was more severe our own casualties heavy. The two machine guns were put out of action, the water jackets being damaged by rifle fire.	The Canal stops A. 1. Walter. Completed by Major R.O.S. Powell Major

INTELLIGENCE SUMMARY

WAR DIARY
or
INTELLIGENCE SUMMARY.
(Erase heading not required.)

Army Form C. 2118.

Hour, Date, Place	Summary of Events and Information	Remarks and references to Appendices
24th 25th & 26th Oct	1st Battalion casualties occurred among the officers. Capt. Reynolds, Lt. Rea killed. Capt. Kennedy died of wounds. Lt. Kenny, 4/Lt. Lavista. 2nd into Magr. (attached) wounded, Major Paunt-concussion. The Battn. which was previously very short handed was now left practically without officers.	Compiled by Major R.H.L. Oswald R. Oswald Major O. 1/Bn. Kennedy since died from his wounds R.H.L.O

(ref: General Ord. of C in C 1st Army METHUNE 29th)

WAR DIARY or INTELLIGENCE SUMMARY.

Army Form C. 2118.

Hour, Date, Place	Summary of Events and Information	Remarks and references to Appendices
3 a.m. 26.X.14 NEUVE-CHAPELLE.	Major DAVNT having gone sick, Captain C.S. Dixon took over command of the Battⁿ. B. Coy in trenches, D Coy in Support. A & C Coys were relieved each unit Billets at RICHEBOURG S^T VAAST. Enemy broke through the line in the vicinity of B & D Coys (commanded by Lieut PINEAU and Lieut INNES-CROSS) no further trace of these Coys or the men commencing them could be obtained. In the afternoon A & C Coys were relieved up into the firing line from RICHEBOURG S^T VAAST. That night the enemy was driven back and A & C Coys re-occupied the trenches. Major J. RYAN D.S.O. R.Munst. Fusiliers took over command of the Battⁿ from Capt. Dixon that evening.	
7 a.m. 27.X.14 NEUVE-CHAPELLE	The trenches to the left of A & C Coys being unoccupied by an on both the enemy about 7 a.m. got round our left flank and rear. After that two Coys had suffered very severe losses from Shrapnel, Howitzer and Rifle fire and Capt. Dixon had sent repeated messages for support, he was obliged to retire three 2 Coys on the village of NEUVE-CHAPELLE (250 yds in rear) to prevent the enemy getting round	

SPLENDID FEAT OF THE ROYAL IRISH RIFLES.

The *Irish Times* says that the officer commanding No. 11 District, Dublin, has received a copy of the following order by the Corps Commander, relating to the Royal Irish Rifles, through the General Officer Commanding 7th Infantry Brigade:—

During an attack by the enemy on the 7th Infantry Brigade last night the enemy came to close quarters with the Royal Irish Rifles, who repulsed them with great gallantry with the bayonet, and made several prisoners. The Corps Commander wishes to compliment the regiment on its splendid feat, and directs that all battalions of the corps shall be informed of the circumstances and of his high appreciation of the gallantry displayed.

Army Form C. 2118.

WAR DIARY
or
INTELLIGENCE SUMMARY.
(Erase heading not required.)

Instructions regarding War Diaries and Intelligence Summaries are contained in F. S. Regs., Part II. and the Staff Manual respectively. Title pages will be prepared in manuscript.

Hour, Date, Place	Summary of Events and Information	Remarks and references to Appendices
11 a.m. 27.X.14 NEUVE-CHAPELLE	in rear of the Brigade. Only 2 Officers and about 46 N.C.O's & men succeeded in getting back out of a total of 5 Officers and about 250 N.C.O's & men. Capt. DAVIS being killed, Lieut. MULCAHY, MORGAN wounded and missing and Capt. JONSSON missing, all these were Special Reserve Officers. The fighting strength of the Battⁿ was now under 200. The Battⁿ that evening went into Billets at RICHEBOURG ST VAAST. Capt. DROUGHT, JONSSON, DAVIS and Lieut ELDRED join. rejoining fourteen joined the Battⁿ	
28.X.14 RICHEBOURG ST VAAST	Battⁿ in Billets.	
4 p.m. 29.X.14 " "	Owing to being heavily shelled by the enemy the Battⁿ moved to LA COUTURE (3 miles) and went into Billets. They were then joined by the remainder of the Brigade.	
30.X.14 LA COUTURE	Capt C.S. DIXON took over command of the Battⁿ from Major RYAN Royal Munster Fusiliers who returned to his Regiment. The Battⁿ marched to DOULIEU (about 12 miles) & lie at once Billeted for the night.	
1 p.m.		
31.X.14 MERRIS	The Battⁿ marched about 6 miles into Billets at MERRIS.	

4

4th Infty Bde. 2nd Bn Royal Irish Rifles

Date	Killed	Officers Wounded	Missing	Other Ranks Killed	Wounded	Missing
12.10.14	Capt G.L. Master			1	7	
13.10.14		2/Lt. Fitzgerald, Capt. H.R. Goodman, C.D. Smyth		2	30	
14.10.14	Lt. B.B. Whitfield	Lt. C. Herron				
15.10.14				3½	47¼	
16.10.14					3	
17.10.14				2	14	
18.10.14				½	2	
21.10.14				1	3	
22.10.14		Capt. H.H. Kennedy		2	24	
26.10.14						

Date	Killed	Wounded	Missing		Killed	Wounded	Missing
	Bt tier						
25.10.14		Capt. J.F. Reynolds	Lt. J. Lowry		73	101	1
		Lt. W.S. Kerr	2/Lt Laville		28	56	
26.10.14							
27.10	1	Capt. Davis	(returning)			20	
			Lt. C.E. Liddely Hope	Capt. A.T. Jonson			
				Lt. H.C. Foley			
				2/Lt. Inclane			
					74	107	320

2nd Batt Royal Irish Rifles

Major R.A.C. Daunt. D.S.O.

Will you kindly complete the attached War Diary for October 1914.

The late Major Alston was prepared to sign it until it was discovered that the dates were incorrect commencing on 14th. Lieut. A.N. Whitfield was killed on 14th.

On last page (25th & 26th Oct.), Capt. Kennedy is shown as Died of Wounds. This should be wounded only, as he died on 24th at BETHUNE.

22nd June 1915.

[signature] Lieutenant,
A/Adjutant, 2nd Bn. Royal Irish Rifles.

Skyolund
2/K.I. Rifles

Man Crawy awarded herewith. I think
the dates are now carried. I am surprised
I hear Capt. Kennedy did not die until Oct 28th.
he was very severely wounded on 20th Oct and
was expected to die very shortly. I am still
under the impression that the M.O. attached to the
Battn informed me on 26th Oct - That Capt Kennedy
was dead.

[signed] Ewart Major
O.C. 2/K.I. Rifles

28-6-15

Major R.A.C. Daunt D.S.O.

      I regret having to return again the attached WarDiary, but it isnecessary that your Initials at least should back each page.   I have had a copy of it made, and the signature is the only thing required on the original.

      Thanking you in anticipation.

                        C. Wakefield, Lieutenant,
                        A/Adjutant, 2nd Bn. Royal Irish Rifles.

16th July 1915.

The Adjutant
2/ R.I. Rifles

Signed as requested.

Daunt Major
Comdg 2/ R.I. Rifles

20/7/15

7th Brigade.
3rd Division.

2nd BATTALION

ROYAL IRISH RIFLES.

NOVEMBER 1 9 1 4.

WAR DIARY or INTELLIGENCE SUMMARY

Instructions regarding War Diaries and Intelligence Summaries are contained in F.S. Regs., Part II. and the Staff Manual respectively. Title pages will be prepared in manuscript.

(Erase heading not required.)

Hour, Date, Place	Summary of Events and Information	Remarks and references to Appendices
1.XI.14 LOCRE (Belgium)	The Battⁿ marched into Billets at LOCRE (9 miles), (Capt CHATTERTON 5 R.I.R. joined the Battⁿ	86
2.XI.14	In Billets. Capts J.P. WHELAN I.R.I.R. and J.C. BROWN R.Inis Inniskillg joined with 40 men joined the Battⁿ	
3.XI.14 "	In Billets. The Battⁿ resting and reorganizing.	
4.XI.14 "	Lieut T.M. MORTON 4 R.I.R. and 40 N.C.O.'s and men joined as 6th Reinforcement. Captain J.B.A. DROGHT 4 R.I.R. was placed on sick list.	
9am 5.XI.14 HOOGE	The Battⁿ marched through YPRES to HOOGE about 4 miles E. of YPRES to relieve the 7th Division in the firing line. (i.e. 7th & 15th Brigades relieved 7th Divⁿ.)	
6.XI.14 HOOGE	The Battⁿ. Heavily shelled about 250 in the trenches	
7.XI.14	In Trenches. Lieut ELDRED dangerously wounded, 3 men killed 14 wounded	
8.XI.14 "	In Support	
9.XI.14 "	In Support	
10.XI.14 "	In Trenches. 1 man killed, 5 wounded.	
11.XI.14 "	In Trenches. Heavy Artillery and Infantry attack by Prussian Guards. 15 killed 10 wounded and 19 missing. The enemy's attack was beaten off with heavy losses to him.	
12.XI.14 "	In Support. 1 man wounded.	
13.XI.14 "	In Support. 4 men wounded.	

INTELLIGENCE SUMMARY.

(Erase heading not required.)

Instructions regarding War Diaries and Intelligence Summaries are contained in F. S. Regs., Part II. and the Staff Manual respectively. Title pages will be prepared in manuscript.

Hour, Date, Place	Summary of Events and Information	Remarks and references to Appendices
14.XI.14. HOOGE	In Brigade Reserve. Fighting Strength of Batt^n 130. 4 men wounded. Capt BROWN James Killing Fusiliers and Lieut MORTON reported sick.	86.
15.XI.14 "	In Brigade Reserve Lieut BARCLAY reported sick.	
16.XI.14 "	In Brigade Reserve Capt G.A. CHATTERTON reported back. 1 Officer and 30 men sent to reinforce WEST KENT Regt.	
17.XI.14 "	In Brigade Reserve 1 Officer and 50 men sent to reinforce K.O.S.B.'s Captain J.P. WHELAN detailed to command 2. SOUTH LANCS and Lieut J. MARTIN to do duty with that Batt^n	
18.XI.14 "	In Brigade Reserve. Batt^n only 40 strong.	
19.XI.14 "	In Brigade Reserve relieved at 7p.m by 5th Fusiliers. 2 men wounded. Spent night in trenches near Divnl H.Q. Quarters about 2 miles E. of YPRES.	
9.a.m 20.XI.14 "	Marched to Brigade H^d Quarters at HOOGE.	
9.30p.m —	The Batt^n marched independently to WESTOUTRE (14 miles)	
3a.m 21.XI.14 WESTOUTRE	In Billets. Capt E.K. CHATTERTON and Mc^LOUGHLIN 3. R.I.R and Lieut S.S. NORMAN 2. R.I.R with a reinforcement of 463 N.C.O.'s and men joined the Batt^n.	
22.XI.14 "	In Billets. The Batt^n resting and reorganising.	

INTELLIGENCE SUMMARY.

(Erase heading not required.)

Hour, Date, Place		Summary of Events and Information	Remarks and references to Appendices
23.11.14	WESTOUTRE	In Billets. L/Cpl Connor was presented on parade by the G.O.C. 3rd Division with the D.C.M. ribbon. C/Sgts HART and GRAY and Sgt BELL promoted 2nd Lieuts from 18.11.14	
24.11.14	"	Captain C.S. Dixon was placed on the sick list and handed over command of the Batt" to Capt J.P. WHELAN.	
25.11.14	"	Major J. Willoughby joined and took over command of the Battalion. Capt Whelan resumed the duties of 2nd in command Bgt. Lieut Davis Browning 2nd B" Munster Fusiliers joined the Battalion for duty.	Jo. 27 =
26.11.14	"	In Billets. A reinforcement of 100 N.C.O.'s & men joined the Battalion	
27.11.14	LOCRE	Marched independently to LOCRE (about 2 miles) and went into billets in support of the trenches	
28.11.14	"	In billets	
29.11.14	"	In billets	
30.11.14	"	"B" went into the trenches near KEMMEL	

7th Brigade.
3rd Division.

2nd BATTALION

ROYAL IRISH RIFLES.

DECEMBER 1914

WAR DIARY
or
INTELLIGENCE SUMMARY.
(Erase heading not required.)

Army Form C. 2118.

Instructions regarding War Diaries and Intelligence Summaries are contained in F.S. Regs., Part II. and the Staff Manual respectively. Title pages will be prepared in manuscript.

Hour, Date, Place	Summary of Events and Information	Remarks and references to Appendices
1. XII. 14. KEMMEL	In the trenches. Casualties 1 man killed and 2 wounded	
2. XII. 14. "	" 1 Cpl and 1 man wounded	
3. XII. 14. "	Relieved from trenches by Royal Scots and marched back to billets at WESTOUTRE (about 7 miles) Casualties 1 Sergt & 1 man killed 3 men wounded	8¢ A
4. XII. 14. WESTOUTRE	In billets in Reserve. [Lutts Gill and Ross]	
5. XII. 14. "	In billets. A reinforcement consisting of Major Tatig C.M.G. D.S.O. 2nd Lieuts R.A. Raymond and C.R. Byat Hardy & 62 N.C.Os and men joined the Battalion. [2nd Lieut Ashfield & Greene proceeded to England on 7 days leave]	
6. XII. 14. "	2nd Lt. E.G. Raymond and 2 Lieut. L.A.G. Greene rejoined Batt." moved to Billets at LOCRE	
7. XII. 14. LOCRE	In billets at LOCRE	
8. XII. 14. "	In billets at LOCRE	
9. XII. 14. "	2nd Lieut. R.B.M.L. returned to field Ambulance and was relieved by Lt. J.A. Wilson. Batt." went into trenches at KEMMEL	

INTELLIGENCE SUMMARY

Army Form C. 2118.

WAR DIARY
or
INTELLIGENCE SUMMARY.
(Erase heading not required.)

Hour, Date, Place	Summary of Events and Information	Remarks and references to Appendices
10. XII. 14. KEMMEL	In trenches. 2 men Rifles 6 wounded	1k w 5 m 1 o 2 k 3
11. XII. 14	Capt. Whelan killed in action [known to have died from wounds received from shrapnel]. Lt. Cameron & Birkbeck wounded from same. Casualties 1 Officer killed, 3 men wounded, 1 missing.	
	In trenches. 1 Rifles 2 wounded. Returned to billets at LOCRE	
13. XII. 14. LOCRE	Draft of 140 men arrived. Report of L. Boyd-Moss L. & billet	86 ?
	It. Colonel R.M.C.B. returned to duty. 2 Riflemen	
	In charge to R.A.M.C. and one other	
	In billet	
14. XII. 14		
15. XII. 14	In billets. Returned to trenches at N. of KEMMEL. 2 men officers 7 wounded	
16. XII. 14 KEARNEY	In trenches. Casualties 6 killed, 7 wounded	
17. XII. 14	In trenches — 3 killed, 4 wounded	
18. XII. 14	In trenches — 3 killed 10 wounded, German bomb busy	
	Relieved at 7 p.m. by R/s R.Ir.Rgt. To LINE at LOCRE	
19. XII. LOCRE	In billets recovering. Lt. Taylor sick to Hospital	
20. XII. 14	In billets. Lt. Thomson sick to Hospital. [Lieut. Gill went to Hospital ill also]	

WAR DIARY
or
INTELLIGENCE SUMMARY.

(Erase heading not required.)

Army Form C. 2118.

Instructions regarding War Diaries and Intelligence Summaries are contained in F. S. Regs., Part II. and the Staff Manual respectively. Title pages will be prepared in manuscript.

Hour, Date, Place	Summary of Events and Information	Remarks and references to Appendices
21. XII. 14 LOCRE	In billets. [Lt Grey & Bell sent on leave to England for 7 days.]	
22. XII. 14	In billets	
23. XII. 14	In billets	
24. XII. 14	In billets, Capt Baker Lt Lucker & 90 men joined.	86
	Battalion to trenches KEMMEL	
25. XII. 14	In trenches. No casualties	
26. XII. 14	In trenches. Casualties 3 wounded	
27. XII. 14 WESTOUTRE	In trenches. Casualties 2 wounded. Marched to WESTOUTRE	
28. XII. 14	In billets.	
29. XII. 14	do.	
30. XII. 14	do. [Jetter Gill rejoined] Lt Thomas sick to hospital	
31. XII. 14	do. Marched to LOCRE	

3RD DIVISION
7TH INFY BDE

2ND BATTALION
ROYAL IRISH RIFLES.
JAN-OCT 1915.

TO 25 DIVISION
74 BRIGADE

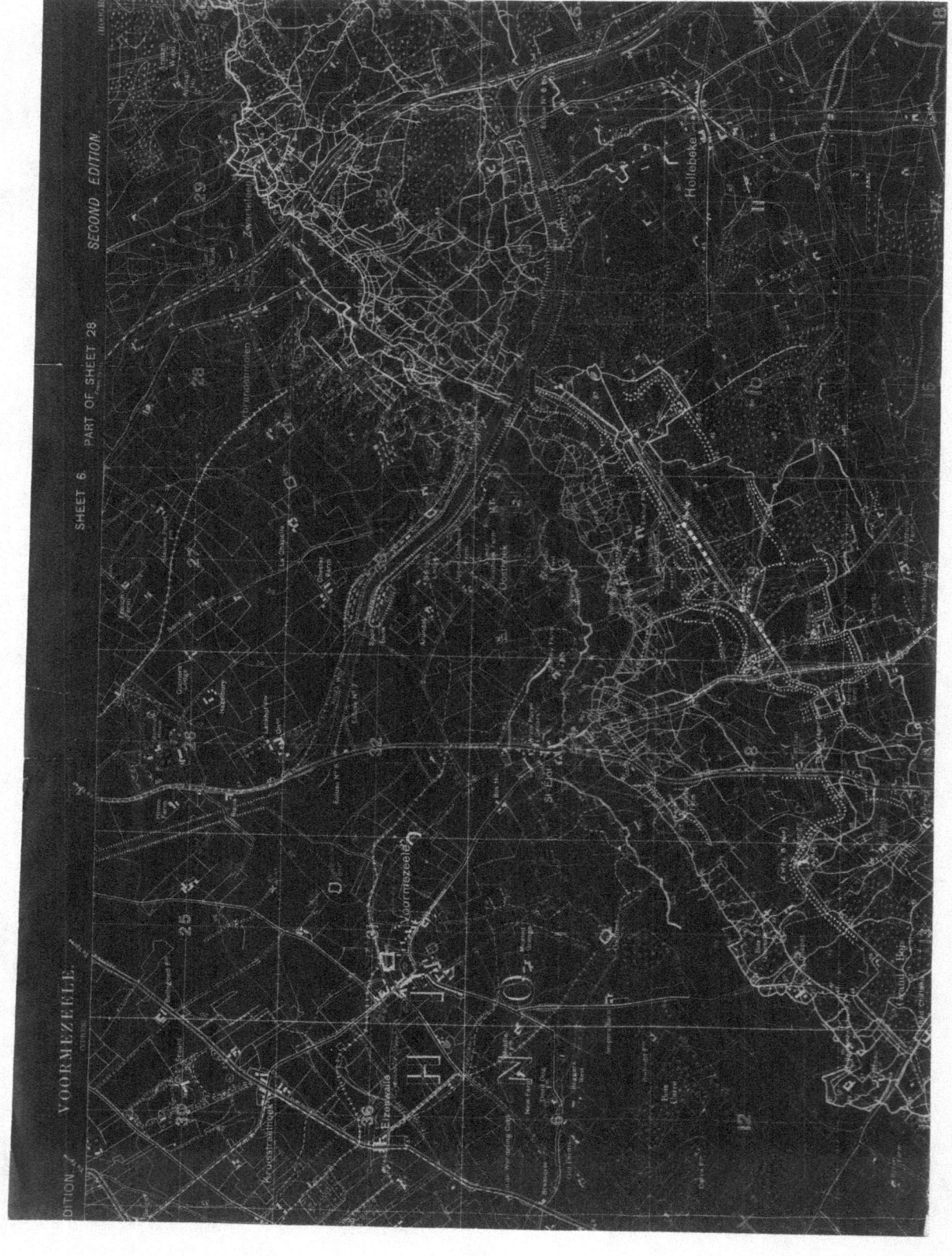

7th Inf.Bde.
3rd Div.

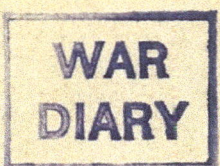

2nd BATTN. THE ROYAL IRISH RIFLES.

J A N U A R Y

1 9 1 5

Army Form C. 2118.

WAR DIARY
or
INTELLIGENCE SUMMARY.
(Erase heading not required.)

Instructions regarding War Diaries and Intelligence Summaries are contained in F. S. Regs, Part II. and the Staff Manual respectively. Title pages will be prepared in manuscript.

Hour, Date, Place	Summary of Events and Information	Remarks and references to Appendices
1. 1. 15. WESTOUTRE	2 killed WESTOUTRE	
2. 1. 15.	do	
3. 1. 15. "	do 2nd Lieut Norman Davis & Ellington (R.A.M.C) joined from leave.	
4. 1. 15. "	Returned to trenches at KEMMEL 2nd Lt Raymond to hospital (sick)	
5. 1. 15. KEMMEL	In trenches. Casualties 1 killed 1 wounded.	
6. 1. 15. "	do Capt. Templeton & Lt Lean joined with 13th reinforcement. Casualties 1 killed 1 wounded.	
7. 1. 15. "	In Trenches. 10 casualties.	
8. 1. 15. "	do Casualties 1 killed 2 wounded. 10 killed	
9. 1. 15. WESTOUTRE	In billets Capt Baker went on leave to England. Lt Luckitt rejoined from hospital.	
10. 1. 15. "	do Major White went on leave to England. Major Lesley in acting in command Capt A. Loughlan Strothers & 150 other ranks to BAILLEUL (Bge H.Q.)	
11. 1. 15. "	do	
12. 1. 15. "	do Returned to trenches near KEMMEL.	
13. 1. 15. KEMMEL	In trenches. 2nd Lt C.L. Pritchard (R.F.R. Rd) attd LI is killed in action. 2 other ranks wounded.	

Army Form C. 2118.

WAR DIARY
or
INTELLIGENCE SUMMARY.
(Erase heading not required.)

Instructions regarding War Diaries and Intelligence Summaries are contained in F.S. Regs., Part II. and the Staff Manual respectively. Title pages will be prepared in manuscript.

Hour, Date, Place			Summary of Events and Information	Remarks and references to Appendices
14 . 1 . 15 .	KEMMEL	L. trenches	Casualties 1 killed	
15 . 1 . 15 .	"	do	1 wounded	
16 . 1 . 15 .	"	do	2 wounded, 1 strayed and found	
			with 14th reinforcement. To billets LOCRE. Sept. back from leave	
17 . 1 . 15 .	LOCRE	L. billets	Major Bleh returned from leave.	
18 . 1 . 15 .	"	do	Dr. Leak to Hospital (sick)	
19 . 1 . 15 .	"	do		
20 . 1 . 15 .	"	do	Returned to trenches near KEMMEL	
21 . 1 . 15 .	KEMMEL	L. trenches	Casualties 1 killed 1 wounded	
22 . 1 . 15 .	"	do	Casualties 3 wounded	
23 . 1 . 15 .	"	do	2 wounded. 15th Reinforcement (95) joined.	
24 . 1 . 15 .	"	do	To billets WESTOUTRE	
25 . 1 . 15 .	WESTOUTRE	L. billets		
26 . 1 . 15 .	"	do		
27 . 1 . 15 .	"	do	L. Col. Shewan & 2/Lieut. Johnston departed with 1	
			D.C.M. Capt Stewart & Capt Gillibrand joined with 16th reinforcement.	

Army Form C. 2118.

WAR DIARY
or
INTELLIGENCE SUMMARY.
(Erase heading not required.)

Instructions regarding War Diaries and Intelligence Summaries are contained in F. S. Regs., Part II. and the Staff Manual respectively. Title pages will be prepared in manuscript.

Hour, Date, Place	Summary of Events and Information	Remarks and references to Appendices
28.1.15. WESTOUTRE	to billets. Returned to trenches near KEMMEL, twenty wounded.	
29.1.15. KEMMEL	In trenches, Sonnette's wounded.	
30.1.15. "	do. 3 killed & wounded, Capt McLaughlin sent to hospital. 14 men sent to division of communication.	
31.1.15. "	In trenches. 2nd Lt Strachan with detachment of 138 return from BAILLEUL to LOCRE. Twenty wounded.	

7th Inf.Bde.
3rd Div.

2nd BATTN. THE ROYAL IRISH RIFLES.

F E B R U A R Y

1 9 1 5

Army Form C. 2118

WAR DIARY
or
INTELLIGENCE SUMMARY.

2/Royal Irish Rifles.

(Erase heading not required.)

February 1915

Instructions regarding War Diaries and Intelligence Summaries are contained in F. S. Regs., Part II. and the Staff Manual respectively. Title pages will be prepared in manuscript.

Place	Date	Hour	Summary of Events and Information	Remarks and references to Appendices
1.	1.II.15.		[KEMMEL] [In trenches] Casualties 9 wounded. Return to Billets LOCRE	
2.	2.II.15		In billets. 17th reinforcement (an O.R.) joined.	
3.	3.II.15		do. Lt. Davis to hospital (sick)	
4.	4.II.15		do	
5.	5.II.15		do. To trenches near KEMMEL (1 signal Corpl Bugg on trans to England. Lt Davies transferred to BETHEM convalescent Depot.	

79
3298

E. Whitton Major
Com.g 2/R.I. Rifles

Army Form C. 2118

WAR DIARY
or
INTELLIGENCE SUMMARY.
(Erase heading not required.)

Instructions regarding War Diaries and Intelligence Summaries are contained in F. S. Regs, Part II. and the Staff Manual respectively. Title pages will be prepared in manuscript.

Hour, Date, Place		Summary of Events and Information	Remarks and references to Appendices
6. II. 15	KEMMEL	In trenches no casualties	
7. II. 15	"	do 2 wounded	
8. II. 15	"	do no casualties	
9. II. 15	"	do 1 wounded	
10. II. 15	WESTOUTRE	In billets. Returned to billets at WESTOUTRE HARTLAND, Rutland & Bence with 10th	
		2nd Lt Agnew, reinforcement of 73 O.R. joined. DAVY	
11. II. 15	"	do Sunday 8 Mainates of H.A. to med w/ from in rotation w/ our Inng, from Lt. Blair, Blatchley, Bland & Bannan. Lt. Colonel Capt, Lieut Young returned to billets.	
12. II. 15	"	do	
13. II. 15	"	do marched to trenches KEMMEL	
14. II. 15	KEMMEL	In trenches 1 man wounded	
15. II. 15	"	do 1 man wounded	

J. Willcocks Major
Comm'g 2/R.I.Rifles

WAR DIARY
or
INTELLIGENCE SUMMARY.
(Erase heading not required.)

Army Form C. 2118

Instructions regarding War Diaries and Intelligence Summaries are contained in F. S. Regs., Part II. and the Staff Manual respectively. Title pages will be prepared in manuscript.

Hour, Date, Place		Summary of Events and Information	Remarks and references to Appendices
16. II. 15	KEMMEL	In trenches. Cpl Ivey H.A.C. (attached to battn) killed our sniper.	
		Sent James Scrivener for bombardment depôt.	
17. II. 15	do	1 other rank killed	
		Casualties 1 killed 2 wounded	
18. II. 15	do	" 1 wounded	
19. II. 15	do	" 6 wounded	
20. II. 15	do	" 4 wounded	
21. II. 15	do	" 2 killed 6 wounded (1 died in hospital Boulogne)	
22. II. 15	do	no casualties. 1 man died of wounds in hospital	
		Returned to billets WESTOUTRE	
23. II. 15	WESTOUTRE	In Billets. 1 died of wounds in hospital	
24. II. 15	do	2 Lts Lyttleton 3rd Regt. Det. Finishing journal	
25. II. 15	do	Cpn H.V. Fell went on leave to England	

J.H. Alston Roger
Com 4/2 R/Rif

WAR DIARY
or
INTELLIGENCE SUMMARY.
(Erase heading not required.)

Army Form C. 2118

Instructions regarding War Diaries and Intelligence Summaries are contained in F. S. Regs., Part II. and the Staff Manual respectively. Title pages will be prepared in manuscript.

Hour, Date, Place	Summary of Events and Information	Remarks and references to Appendices
26.II.15 WESTOUTRE	2 Lt R.R.L., 2 Lt K.L. Godson found, 2 Lt S.B. Bullock & hospital sick. To trenches KEMMEL.	
27.II.15 KEMMEL	2 Lt trenches, Casualties 2 wounded, 1 died of wounds in hospital. Major Leatham & Capt Myers to base & ENGLAND	
28.II.15 "	do 3 wounded. Ordered of wounds in hospital. 2 Lt G.W. Webb and 61 other ranks (1st Rumford ment) joined	
24.II.15 do		J.H.Lloyd Byron Lieut & A.J.Regt.

79
3298

7th Inf.Bde.
3rd Div.

2nd BATTN. THE ROYAL IRISH RIFLES.

M A R C H

1 9 1 5

Army Form C. 21

WAR DIARY
or
INTELLIGENCE SUMMARY.
(Erase heading not required.)

Instructions regarding War Diaries and Intelligence Summaries are contained in F. S. Regs., Part II. and the Staff Manual respectively. Title pages will be prepared in manuscript.

Hour, Date, Place	Summary of Events and Information	Remarks and references to Appendices

1. 7.II.15. KEMMEL — 2 men killed 4 wounded

2. " " — do — 1 Officer (2 Lt J.C. Sparkes) Reg. Adj. Sec.) & 2 men killed 4 wounded. [2nd R.I.R. to new hospital at ...]

3. 8.II.15 " — do — 4 wounded. Officer reported to R. Buie (M.A.C.) Hospital and...

4. 9.II.15 " — do — Returned to billets WESTOUTRE. [2 Lt Brown returned from hospital]

5. 10.II.15 WESTOUTRE — 3 killed — 6 N.C.O. candidates to be sent to School BAILLEUL [Sgts Oakford, Kahn, Chapman, Bowman Bletchley and Bland]

6. 11.II.15 " — do —

7. 12.II.15 " — do — Lieut (temp) L.S. Ellington M.O. transferred to BERTHEN Lieut Q.R.J. healey A.R.M.C. posted as M.O. on full returned from leave

WAR DIARY
or
INTELLIGENCE SUMMARY.
(Erase heading not required.)

Army Form C. 2118

Instructions regarding War Diaries and Intelligence Summaries are contained in F.S. Regs., Part II. and the Staff Manual respectively. Title pages will be prepared in manuscript.

Hour, Date, Place	Summary of Events and Information	Remarks and references to Appendices
8. III.15 WESTOUTRE	Lt. Little (2nd Mgred. regiment) see hour Regimental orders wrote II on amount of photographs and certificate to 15.3.15	
9. III.15 "	2 killed	
10. III.15 "	2 killed	
11. III.15 "	1 killed. 2 others gone to hospital sick	
12. III.15 " 2.30 a.m.	Assault of LINDENHOEK and was held in reserve while an attack was made on SPANBROEK FARM by the Worcester & Wilts. Regt. The enemy's trenches were captured but could not be held. The battalion had no casualties, and returned to original billets after dark. (Owing to the thick mist the attack which was timed to take place in the early morning was postponed till 4.10 p.m.)	
13. III.15 " 8.30 a.m.	Battalion marched off to take over a new line of trenches near DRANOUTRE, but the order was cancelled just after the trenches were reached and the battalion returned to DRANOUTRE and went into billets late at night. the 28th Brigade is 2nd Div (ARMY) Reserve, marge.	86

WAR DIARY
or
INTELLIGENCE SUMMARY.

(Erase heading not required.)

Army Form C. 2118

Instructions regarding War Diaries and Intelligence Summaries are contained in F. S. Regs., Part II. and the Staff Manual respectively. Title pages will be prepared in manuscript.

Hour, Date, Place		Summary of Events and Information	Remarks and references to Appendices
14.III.15	DRANOUTRE 12 noon	L. Billets. The Battalion returned to the former billets at WESTOUTRE	
15.III.15	WESTOUTRE	L. Billets	
16.III.15	"	L. Billets. The battalion moved in evening to huts at LOCRE	
17.III.15	LOCRE	L. huts. The battalion goes into trenches near KEMMEL	
18.III.15	KEMMEL	L. trenches & trenches. 1 killed 3 wounded.	
19.III.15	"	do 8 wounded	
20.III.15	"	do 1 killed 9 wounded	86 Fla
21.III.15	"	do 2 killed	
22.III.15	"	do 3 wounded	
23.III.15	"	do 1 killed 4 wounded (2nd Lieut Bulled slightly) 2nd Lt C. HEALES was taken to hospital when dangerously ill	
		Battery marched to billets at LA CLYTTE	

WAR DIARY
       ## or
       ## INTELLIGENCE SUMMARY.
       (Erase heading not required.)

Army Form C. 2118

Hour, Date, Place	Summary of Events and Information	Remarks and references to Appendices
24.III.15. LA CLYTTE	2 Lieut. A. E. Falkiner returned from hospital.	
25.III.15 "	do. [2nd Lieut. J.W. Stacey W.J. Stacey] 2/Lt remain in Royal Dublin transferred [but the two foregoing were retained to join the 1st Battn at once]	
26.III.15. "	do Nothing to record. CB.	
27 Mar 1915 "	" Nothing to record. CB.	
28th " " "	" LT D.M. ANDERSON 5TH BN R.I. RIFLES and 2/LT A.L. BAKER R. DUB. FUS. joined for duty with the Battalion.	CB.
29th " " "	" until the evening, when the Battn marched to ELZENWALLE and went into trenches near St ELOI. (Ref. MAP. BELGIUM. SHEET 28. H:36c)	CB.
30TH " " ELZENWALLE	In trenches — CASUALTIES 2 wounded.	CB.
31st " " "	In trenches — (2/LT B.E. WHITMORE joined the Bn for duty) CASUALTIES. 2 wounded	CB.

7th Inf. Bde.
3rd Div.

2nd BATTN. THE ROYAL IRISH RIFLES.

A P R I L

1 9 1 5

Army Form C. 2118

WAR DIARY
or
INTELLIGENCE SUMMARY.
(Erase heading not required.)

Instructions regarding War Diaries and Intelligence Summaries are contained in F.S. Regs., Part II. and the Staff Manual respectively. Title pages will be prepared in manuscript.

Hour, Date, Place	Summary of Events and Information	Remarks and references to Appendices
1915	MAP REFERENCES:- BELGIUM. SHEET 28: 1/40,000.	
1ST APRIL: ELZENWALLE (H.36.c) In trenches.	2/LT JOY R.I.RIFLES and 36 other ranks joined the BN for duty.	20TH Reinforcement &c.
	2/LT G.W.CALVERLEY 2/R.I.RIFLES and 2/LT A.L.BAKER 3/R.DUB.FUS.(att) to Hosp^l (Sick)	&c.
	CASUALTIES: 1 Killed. 1 wounded.	
2ND APRIL "	In Trenches. LT. P.J.L. DAVIES 4/MUNS.FUS. and 2/LT R.B. HAYWARD 2/R.I.RIFLES to Hospital (Sick)	&c.
	CASUALTIES: 2. Killed. 3 wounded.	
3RD APRIL "	In trenches. CASUALTIES: 4 wounded	&c.
4TH APRIL "	In trenches.	&c.
5TH APRIL. LA CLYTTE (N.7.c)	To billets at LA CLYTTE (N.7.C)	
	In billets. LT. R.B. HUTCHESON 2/R.I.RIFLES rejoined the Batt^n for duty. 2/LT K.L. GODSON 2/R.I.RIFLES to Hospital (Sick) Battalion employed at night trench digging near Bois CARRÉ (N.12.B)	&c.
6TH APRIL "	In billets. Reinforcement of 31 N.C.O's & R'men arr^d	21st Reinforcement &c.
7TH APRIL "	In billets.	
8TH " "	In billets.	
9TH " "	In billets.	

Army Form C. 2118

WAR DIARY
or
INTELLIGENCE SUMMARY.
(Erase heading not required.)

Instructions regarding War Diaries and Intelligence Summaries are contained in F. S. Regs., Part II. and the Staff Manual respectively. Title pages will be prepared in manuscript.

Hour, Date, Place 1915	Summary of Events and Information MAP REFERENCES:- BELGIUM. SHEET 28. 1/40,000.	Remarks and references to Appendices
APRIL 10TH LA CLYTTE (N.7.C)	In billets until the evening, where the Battalion marched to trenches between ST ELOI and KEMMEL. CASUALTIES - NIL.	C.B.
APRIL 11TH VIERSTRAAT or DICKEBUSCH AREA. ELZENWALLE (H.30.c.c)	In trenches [CASUALTIES 2/Lt.C.R.E.LITTLEDALE 3/R.DUB.FUS. and 3 others wounded] 73 other ranks joined	C.B. 22nd Reinforcement. C.B.
APRIL 12TH N.12.d "	In trenches (2/Lt J.G.BLAND joined for duty. CASUALTIES. 1(w) a ZEPPELIN AIRSHIP passed over trenches at 11.30.p.m. Steering a S.W. course	C.B.
APRIL 13TH "	In trenches: CASUALTIES. 1 KILLED, 4 wounded	C.B.
APRIL 14TH "	In trenches: CASUALTIES: 5 wounded.	C.B.
APRIL 15TH "	In trenches: At 3.30 A.M on this date MAJ.J.W.ALSTON (Comm.g the Battn) proceeded to the trenches for the day, to observe the enemy's position. At 5.p.m while observing with a trench periscope, a bullet obviously aimed for the top glass of the periscope struck a sandbag on the parapet and, being deflected, struck the MAJOR in the head above the left ear. He never recovered consciousness or spoke, and died at 5.15 p.m. CASUALTIES (OTHER RANKS) 1(K) 3(W) CAPT.C.M.L.BECHER assumed command of the BATTALION.	[killed] C.B.
APRIL 16TH "	In trenches: CASUALTIES. 10(W). At night to huts at DICKEBUSCH	C.B.

WAR DIARY
or
INTELLIGENCE SUMMARY.

(Erase heading not required.)

Army Form C. 2118

Hour, Date, Place 1915.	Summary of Events and Information	Remarks and references to Appendices
	MAP REFERENCES:- BELGIUM. SHEET 28; 1/40,000.	
APRIL 17TH DICKEBUSCH	Battalion in huts. 2/LT W.E. ANDREWS, 3/R.I. RIFLES joined for duty. R'man DORAN (wounded yesterday) died of wounds. MAJOR J.W. ALSTON who died in the C of E. burial ground. Sgt DICKE- BUSCH CHURCH, WITH MILITARY HONOURS.	CA.
APRIL 18TH "	In huts: 9 Machine gunners from 3/R.B. joined for duty and were posted to "C" Coy.	CA.
APRIL 19TH "	In huts.	
APRIL 20TH "	In huts. At 6.15 p.m. the Battn. paraded and marched to trenches in last position, relieving the 3RD WORCESTERSHIRE REGT. CASUALTIES 1(K) 1(W) Notification received this day that MAJOR A.V. WEIR 1ST BN. had been posted to the Command of this Battn.	CB.
APRIL 21ST VIERSTRAAT AREA N.12.d	In trenches: CASUALTIES. 1(K) 1 OFFR (CAPT V.K. GILLILAND) and 7 other ranks (W) 2 injured by enemy's artillery. Sandbags displaced by enemy's artillery. 15 N.C.O.s + men joined the BN for duty.	23rd Reinforcement. CA.
APRIL 22ND "	In trenches, CASUALTIES — 1(W).	CA.
APRIL 23RD "	In Trenches	CA.
APRIL 24TH "	2/LT E.J. HOARE rejoined the Bn for duty, on return from M.G. course. CASUALTIES. 6 (W)	CA.
APRIL 25TH "	In trenches CASUALTIES — 2 (W). 70 N.C.O.s + R'men joined for duty this day. Battn (relieved by 3rd WORCS. REGT) returns to Huts (DICKEBUSCH)	24TH REINFORCEMENT. CB.

WAR DIARY
or
INTELLIGENCE SUMMARY.
(Erase heading not required.)

Army Form C. 2118

Instructions regarding War Diaries and Intelligence Summaries are contained in F. S. Regs., Part II. and the Staff Manual respectively. Title pages will be prepared in manuscript.

MAP REFERENCES:- BELGIUM SHEET 28: 1/40,000.

Hour, Date, Place	Summary of Events and Information	Remarks and references to Appendices
1915		
APRIL 26TH DICKEBUSCH	In "CANADA" huts. An enemy's aeroplane passed over the huts occupied by the Bn this day, and 5 bombs were dropped resulting in 17 CASUALTIES (W) of which 14 went to United to Hospital, and 3 being only slightly wounded remained at duty. 300 men were employed on digging a new fire trench at night. 7/9 fatigue	C2.
APRIL 27TH DICKEBUSCH	300 men of Bn employed on digging fatigue near fire trenches at night. CASUALTIES: 1 (K) & 1 (W).	C3.
APRIL 28TH DICKEBUSCH	MAJOR A.V. WEIR. 1ST Bn joined this day & took over command of the Bn from CAPT C.M.L. BECHER.	C2.
APRIL 29TH DICKEBUSCH	2nd Lieut C.H WALE from QUEEN VICTORIA RIFLES joined the Battalion.	CASUALTIES DURING MONTH OF APRIL OFFICERS K. 2. W. 5. INJURED N.C.O's + R'MEN. 9. 65. - 2.
APRIL 30TH DICKEBUSCH	The Battalion relieved the 3rd WORCESTERS in the trenches this night. No casualties.	REINFORCEMENTS OFFICERS — 5 N.C.O's + R'MEN 234.

J V Weir Major
Cmdg 2. Royal Ir. Rifles

7th Inf.Bde.
3rd Div.

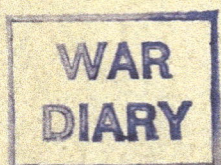

2nd BATTN. THE ROYAL IRISH RIFLES.

M A Y

1 9 1 5

WAR DIARY
INTELLIGENCE SUMMARY.

Army Form C. 2118.

Hour, Date, Place	Summary of Events and Information	Remarks and references to Appendices
1915		
MAY 1st VIERSTRAAT AREA N12A	West B. E. L. G. I. U. M. gz. 28 4D. [?]. In the trenches. A good deal of rifle & shelling from both sides. No casualties. Captain C. Farren 3rd Royal Irish Rifles & 25 other ranks joined as 1st reinforcement.	
MAY 2nd "	In the trenches. Trenches shelled. Enemy as usual. Fire for 3 half hours. Casualties killed 6 Riflemen wounded 29 Riflemen. Rapid fire which knocked about Rifle[?] brigade & an[?] quiet.	Weather very hot. Q? from "Smoke Flo-Sand[?] G.O.C.
MAY 3rd "	In the trenches. Trenches shelled again in early afternoon shell fire our side at mid day and again at 5.30 p.m. Casualties killed 2 Rifle[?] man wounded 13 Riflemen.	
MAY 4th "	In the trenches fairly quiet day. One mild shell near H.Q. 94 from the enemy. Relieved by 2nd Worcesters. A.B.C. Coys to DICKEBUSCH. D. Coy in reserve RIDGE WOOD. H.Q.s. DICKEBUSCH.	

WAR DIARY
or
INTELLIGENCE SUMMARY.
(Erase heading not required.)

Army Form C. 2118.

Instructions regarding War Diaries and Intelligence Summaries are contained in F. S. Regs., Part II. and the Staff Manual respectively. Title pages will be prepared in manuscript.

Hour, Date, Place	Summary of Events and Information	Remarks and references to Appendices
1915 MAY 6th DICKE-BUSCH.	Map BELGIUM Sheet 28 1/40,000. Ordered to move at 3 p.m. to join 13th Bde. Moved to point near HILL 60 & relieved BEDFORD REGT. (4 guns were not sent as the front line and were not well acquainted with the route) the relief was not complete till 2.30 a.m.	
MAY 7th YPRES	D Coy on right of our sector were ordered to join in attack on Hill 60 with 2 Coys to assist the Bedfords in an advance. Communication trench partly blown in — Hun partially destroyed — Their fire from the hill was heavy. Officers were met casualties Captain G.A. BURGOYNE (slight) and Lieut. P.A. LEASK (slight) also 2 wounded other ranks 9 killed 16 wounded. Attack failed. A good deal of shelling. In hospital breakdown & Captain R.B. HUTCHESON	

WAR DIARY or INTELLIGENCE SUMMARY.

Army Form C. 2118.

MAP BELGIUM SHEETS 28 & HOOGE

Hour, Date, Place	Summary of Events and Information	Remarks and references to Appendices
1915		
MAY 8TH YPRES - HILL 60	Trenches bombed by enemy. Casualties Captain V.K. GILLILAND killed. 2nd Lieut. G.N. WEBB wounded. Other ranks killed & wounded 8. Withdrew to trenches at HOOGE. (Spent good night there. 9.5.15 fired on our billets).	
MAY 9TH "	Trenches bombed & shelled heavily by enemy. 6 platoon trench destructed to hold enemy. Casualties killed 3 wounded 21. Retain amount. L't Shirley Severn J. ffrench killed. Battn Hdqrs + Reg'l AID POST. billets C/3.	
MAY 10TH "	Trenches fairly quiet. 2 Limbers to parapets Lt.-G.S. NORMAN to hospital Concussion (W). Casualties killed 1 wounded —	
MAY 11TH "	Trenches bombed & fired on by enemy. Party of enemy party who had tried a will rapid fire. 5 dead left in front. RAYMOND reported. (1 killed 5 wounded of ours)	

(9 26 6) W 257—976 100,000 4/12 H W V 3298 79

WAR DIARY
or
INTELLIGENCE SUMMARY.

(Erase heading not required.)

Army Form C. 2118.

Instructions regarding War Diaries and Intelligence Summaries are contained in F.S. Regs., Part II. and the Staff Manual respectively. Title pages will be prepared in manuscript.

Hour, Date, Place	Summary of Events and Information	Remarks and references to Appendices
	MAP BELGIUM Sheet 28 H.B.000	
1915 MAY 12th LA CLYTTE DICKEBUSCH	Battn relieved 1/2 Royal Scots. Relief in full 2am. Reinforcement 40 8th ranks joined. Casualties 3 wounded byreliefs	28th Reinforcement
MAY 13th. LACLYTTE	In huts at LA CLYTTE	
MAY 14th " "	In huts	
MAY 15th " "	In huts. Captain E.C. MAYNE left to join 1st Battn	
MAY 16 " "	In huts. Batt'n paraded at 7.30 p - Relieved 3rd WORCESTERS - trenches no casualties during relief.	
MAY 17th VIERSTRAAT dug in N.2.d	In trenches shown on map. one killed	
MAY 18th " "	In trenches some shelling 6 men wounded	
MAY 19th " "	Some shelling of the German new reply to our shells. own guns fired two shortfalling and wounding (four)(5) Parts of shell returned to battery. no other casualties	

WAR DIARY
or
INTELLIGENCE SUMMARY.
(Erase heading not required.)

Army Form C. 2118.

Instructions regarding War Diaries and Intelligence Summaries are contained in F. S. Regs, Part II. and the Staff Manual respectively. Title pages will be prepared in manuscript.

Hour, Date, Place 1915.	Summary of Events and Information	Remarks and references to Appendices
MAY 20TH VIERSTRAAT N.12.d	MAP BELGIUM Sheet 28 H/9000 Bath relieved French by 3rd WORCESTERS & returned to DICKEBUSCH at 12 midnight. Quiet day, no casualties	&c.
MAY 21ST DICKEBUSCH Farms.	A + C Coy. in CANADA HUTS, B + D Coy in Farms.	&c.
MAY 22nd "	Billets as above.	&c.
MAY 23rd "	" "	&c.
MAY 24th "	" " The farm occupied by "D" Coy was shelled at about noon. Casualties K.5. W.11. Reinforcement 27TH REINFORCEMENT of 22 Riflemen joined (no officers) + no N.C.O.'s	&c.
MAY 25TH VIERSTRAAT AREA (N.12.d.)	The Battalion paraded at 8 p.m. & proceeded to trenches in the usual area, relieving the 3/WORCS. In trenches. Usual amount of sniping. Casualties W.4.	&c.
" 26th "	: No casualties	&c.
" 27th "	: Casualties from sniping K.2. W.1.	&c.
" 28th "	. A little shelling — no casualties	&c.
" 29th "	: A quiet day. Casualties 1 W	&c.

Army Form C. 2118.

WAR DIARY
or
INTELLIGENCE SUMMARY.
(Erase heading not required.)

Instructions regarding War Diaries and Intelligence Summaries are contained in F.S. Regs., Part II. and the Staff Manual respectively. Title pages will be prepared in manuscript.

Hour, Date, Place 1915	Summary of Events and Information	Remarks and references to Appendices
	MAP REFERENCES:- BELGIUM. SHEET 28. 1/40000.	
MAY 30TH VIERSTRAAT AREA. (N.12d.)	In Trenches. Parapets damaged by shell fire. No casualties. Major A.V. WEIR proceeded to Bde H.Qs this morning to take over the post of Commandant of 7TH Bde AREAS, handing over command of the BATTN to CAPT C.M.L. BECHER	C3.
MAY 31ST " "	In Trenches. Quiet day. No casualties. 2/LIEUT OSCAR FAYLE 4TH R.I.RIFLES joined the Bn for duty and was posted to "B" COY	C3.
		CASUALTIES DURING MONTH OF MAY. OFFICERS K-- W=5 1 - 4 - 1. N.C.Os & R'MEN 36 - 120. 68. REINFORCEMENTS. OFFICERS. 2 N.C.Os & R'MEN 87.

CBecher. Capt.
Comm'g 2/R.I.Rifles.
31st May 1915.

7th Inf.Bde.
3rd Div.

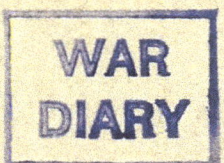

2nd BATTN. THE ROYAL IRISH RIFLES.

J U N E

1 9 1 5

WAR DIARY
or
INTELLIGENCE SUMMARY.

(Erase heading not required.)

Army Form C. 2

MAP REFERENCES:- BELGIUM. SHEET 28. 1/40,000.

Place		Summary of Events and Information	Remarks and references to Appendices
VIERSTRAAT AREA (N.12.d)	In trenches.	Casualties (Stray Shots) 3 W. MAJOR E.M. MORRIS (DEVONSHIRE REGT) arrived this day and took over Command of the Bat:- from CAPT. BECHER	
"	"	Enemy quiet along our front. Casualties - 1.K. Lieut. W.E.S. Howard, 2nd Lieut. A. Ferris, & G.G.M. Bennett, 4th Bn. R. Irish Rifles, joined the Battalion for duty.	
"	"	A little shelling on both sides. Very slight damage to our line. Casualties - 2.W. 2nd Lieut. A. Ferris, 4th R. Ir. Rif. to Hospital, sick. The Battalion was relieved by units of the 85th Infantry Brigade (East Surrey, Middlesex Regt. Royal Fusiliers), and marched to Bivouac near to and S.W. of VLAMERTINGHE - POPERINGHE Road	
"		In Bivouac as above.	

WAR DIARY
or
INTELLIGENCE SUMMARY.

(Erase heading not required.)

Army Form C. 2118

Hour, Date, Place	Summary of Events and Information	Remarks and references to Appendices
1915	MAP REFERENCES – BELGIUM – SHEET 28. 1/40,000	
June, 5th. In bivouac.	A party of 9 officers and 400 N.C.O's and men, was furnished to carry barbed wire entanglements to YPRES Salient. Lieut. A.R.D. Carberry, R.A.M.C. proceeded to join 8th Field Ambulance for duty. Lieut. C. Jacob, R.A.M.C. joined in relief.	
June, 6th. "	A party of 5 officers and 200 N.C.O's & men proceeded with barbed wire entanglements to YPRES Salient.	
June, 7th. "	Another party as above, performed the same duty.	
June, 8th. "	Moved into a bivouac about 300 yards WEST of old camp. The Commanding Officer, Adjutant, Machine Gun Officer and two officers per company visited the new line of trenches to be taken over by the battalion at HOOGE. One officer of each company and the Machine Gun Officer remained in the trenches overnight.	

Army Form C. 2118.

WAR DIARY
or
INTELLIGENCE SUMMARY.
(Erase heading not required.)

Hour, Date, Place	Summary of Events and Information	Remarks and references to Appendices
	MAP REFERENCES - BELGIUM - SHEET 28 $\frac{1}{40,000}$	
1915 June 9th	In Bivouac	2nd Lieut. B.E. Whitmore to Hospital, sick. The Battalion paraded at 7 pm and proceeded to the trenches at HOOGE, relieving the 3rd Worcestershire Regt. Casualties - 1. W.
June 10th	In trenches, HOOGE	Casualties - 2 wounded.
June 11th	" "	Casualties - 1 Killed, 9 wounded. The Battalion was relieved by Northumberland Fusiliers (149th Brigade), with the exception of "B" Company, a party of "C" Company attached and the Machine Gun team (about 250 all ranks) who had to remain, owing to the late arrival of relieving unit, and the impossibility of getting clear of the trenches before daylight. Batt. proceeded to Bivouac vacated on June 9th. Re-inforcement of 18 Other Ranks joined Battalion.
June 12th	In Bivouac	10951 L/Sergt. J.M. McIntosh, promoted 2nd Lieut. dated 27.5.15 and posted to "C" Company for duty.

Army Form C. 2118.

WAR DIARY
or
INTELLIGENCE SUMMARY.
(Erase heading not required.)

Summary of Events and Information

MAP REFERENCES — BELGIUM, SHEET 28 — 1/40,000.

Hour, Date, Place 1915.		Remarks and References to Appendices
June, 12th (continued)	2nd Lieut. G.S. Coomber, R. Irish Fusiliers, joined for duty and posted to "C" Company. "B" Company, details of "C" Coy. and Machine Gun teams, relieved from the trenches and reached bivouac about Mid-night. Casualties — 1 killed, 7 wounded.	
June 13th	In bivouac.	
June 14th	" . Officers lectured by 2nd in Command on Fetking's Regulations. Copies of the Corps Commander's message complimenting the Battalion on the gallantry displayed in October last at NEUVE CHAPELLE, when it repulsed the enemy with the bayonet, were distributed to companies and read out on parade. Sports were held in the afternoon. The principal event was the High Jump for the Commanding Officer's prize. This was won by a jump of 4'9½".	
June 15th	In bivouac. The Battalion paraded at 5.30 pm and marched to	

WAR DIARY
or
INTELLIGENCE SUMMARY.
(Erase heading not required.)

Army Form C. 2118

Instructions regarding War Diaries and Intelligence Summaries are contained in F. S. Regs., Part II. and the Staff Manual respectively. Title pages will be prepared in manuscript.

Hour, Date, Place	Summary of Events and Information	Remarks and References to Appendices
	MAP REFERENCES - BELGIUM, SHEET 28, 1/40,000	
1915		
June 15th (contd)	to the Assembly trenches between WITTEPOORT FARM and Railway to support 9th Infantry Brigade in an attack on BELLEWAARDE SPUR. Strength:- 21 Officers, 630 other ranks.	
June 16th	The bombardment by our Artillery commenced at 2.50 A.M., lasting until 4.15 A.M., when the 9th Infantry Brigade assaulted, carrying the first three lines of German trenches. The 2nd R. Irish Rifles supported the left - "C" Company followed by "D" Company on right, "A" Coy followed by "B" Company on left, with orders to consolidate the first German line. "C" and "D" Companies, carried away by their keenness, pushed through to the 3rd line, closing up with the assaulting troops under Captain E.C. FARRAN & Lieutenant C.H.H. EALES. These companies were then re-organised and withdrawn in perfect order to the first line, which they put in a state of defence. "A" Company, under 2nd Lieut. W.E Andrews was similarly engaged on the left. Owing	

(3 29 6) W 2794 100,000 8/14 H W V Forms/C. 2118/11.

Army Form C. 2118.

WAR DIARY
or
INTELLIGENCE SUMMARY.
(Erase heading not required.)

Hour, Date, Place	Summary of Events and Information	Remarks and References to Appendices
	MAP REFERENCES - BELGIUM SHEET 28. 40,000.	
June 16th (cont'd) 1915	Owing to heavy Artillery fire which soon developed, "B" Company was unable to follow "A" Coy quickly. They were formed up on CAMBRIDGE Road 250 yards behind, preparatory to making another effort to get through, when they were unfortunately shelled by enfilade fire causing 30 or 40 casualties. The remainder of the Company was then withdrawn and kept in battalion support for the remainder of the day. During the day, from early morning to nightfall the Battalion was subjected to a terrific artillery bombardment. The Non-commissioned Officers and men of all Companies distinguished themselves by their discipline, coolness, and steadiness under most trying circumstances. At no time during the day could it be said that they were in any way shaken by their ordeal. For instance, at 3-30 pm, after hours of bombardment, "C"	

Army Form C. 2118.

WAR DIARY
or
INTELLIGENCE SUMMARY.
(Erase heading not required.)

Instructions regarding War Diaries and Intelligence Summaries are contained in F. S. Regs., Part II. and the Staff Manual respectively. Title pages will be prepared in manuscript.

Hour, Date, Place	Summary of Events and Information	Remarks and References to Appendices
1915	MAP REFERENCES – BELGIUM – SHEET 28. 1/40,000	
June 16th	"C" and "D" Companies, with very short notice, were called upon to attack. It possessed just so much spirit and dash as their early morning attack. Both of these attacks were gallantly led by Captain E.C. EARRAN, who was wounded and became missing, and 2nd Lieut. C.H.H. EALES, who was uninjured.	
	"A" Company consolidated and held, in a most determined manner, the left flank of the German trenches and handed them over intact to the Royal Scots who relieved them at midnight. 2nd Lieut. W.E. Andrews, who commanded this portion of the line deserves the highest praise for the able way in which this difficult operation was carried out. The Battalion was relieved at 1-29 AM, having acquitted itself in a manner which has called forth praise from the Corps Commander, the following	
June 16–17th		

Army Form C. 2118.

WAR DIARY
or
INTELLIGENCE SUMMARY.
(Erase heading not required.)

Hour, Date, Place	Summary of Events and Information	Remarks and References to Appendices
1915	MAP REFERENCES — BELGIUM, SHEET 28, 1/40,000	
16th/17th June	Following officers and about 300 Other ranks became casualties:—	
	Capt. C.M.L. BECHER, slightly wounded.	
	" E.C. FARRAN, 3rd R. Ir. Rifles. Wounded and Missing.	
	Lieut. W.E.S. HOWARD, 4th " Wounded	
	" D.M. ANDERSON, 5th " " "	
	2nd Lt. E.J. HOARE " "	
	" J.G. BLAND " "	
	" F.C.P. JOY, 3rd R. Ir. Rifles. KILLED.	
	" E.B. KERTLAND, 4/R. Irish Fus., Wounded and Missing.	
	" R.L. VANCE, 4/R. Irish Fus., Wounded	
	" T.J. CONSIDINE, 5/R. Dub. Fus., Wounded	
	" C.H. WALE, Special List, Wounded	
	" J.M. McINTOSH, KILLED	
	" A.A. RAYMOND, slightly wounded, remained at duty.	
17th June	In Bivouac near VLAMERTINGHE – POPERINGHE Road	

Army Form C. 2118.

WAR DIARY
or
INTELLIGENCE SUMMARY.
(Erase heading not required.)

MAP REFERENCES – BELGIUM – SHEET 28 $\frac{1}{40,000}$

Hour, Date, Place 1915	Summary of Events and Information	Remarks and References to Appendices
17th June 1915	Captain H.R. Goodman joined the Battalion	
18th June	In bivouac as above	
19th June	do	
20th June	Captain C.M.L. Becher to Hospital, wounded. Battalion marched to Dug-out, Square H.11.D. Headquarters in Farm House.	
21st June	In dugouts as above	
22nd June	— do —	
23rd June	— do — Major E.M. Morris promoted Lieut Colonel of 2nd Bn the King's Own (Royal Lancaster Regt) and left to join his new unit. The following farewell order was published by him "Lieutenant Colonel E.M. Morris, in giving up command of the 2nd Bn the Royal Irish Rifles on promotion to command the King's Own (Royal Lancaster Regiment) wishes the 2nd Bn the Royal Irish Rifles every good luck and success now and at all times. He	

WAR DIARY or INTELLIGENCE SUMMARY.

Army Form C. 2118.

(Erase heading not required.)

Hour, Date, Place 1915	Summary of Events and Information	Remarks and References to Appendices
	MAP REFERENCES - BELGIUM. SHEET 28. 1/40,000	
23rd June	He also wishes to sincerely thank all ranks for their support and assistance, during his short period of Command, and begs them never to forget NEUVE CHAPELLE, and BELLEWAARDE FARM on the 16th instant, when on both occasions their battalion covered themselves with glory." Capt. H.R. Goodman took over Command of the Battn. The Battalion marched to the trenches (B.8. & B.9.) near HOOGE and relieved the 3rd Worcestershire Regiment. 2nd Lieut. G.S. COOMBER, Royal Scots Fus, to hospital sick. Casualties - 1 Other rank wounded.	
24th June	In trenches. 2nd Lieut. C.H.H.EALES, to Hospital, sick. Major G.A.WEIR, D.S.O., 3rd Dragoon Guards joined the Battn. and assumed command. Casualties. O.R. 2 W.	
25th June	In trenches. Casualties - O.R. 2 W. 2nd Lieut. C.F. Wilkins joined with a re-inforcement of 142 O.Ranks (included 18 Mr. Gunners & 12 Signallers).	

WAR DIARY
or
INTELLIGENCE SUMMARY.
(Erase heading not required.)

Army Form C. 2118.

Hour, Date, Place	Summary of Events and Information	Remarks and References to Appendices
1915	MAP REFERENCES - BELGIUM - SHEET 28, 1/40,000	
25th June	The Reinforcement remained with Transports until return of Battalion from the trenches.	
26th June	In trenches. A little shelling by enemy along our line.	
27th June	A portion of the parapet and parados of B.9 damaged. A fair amount of shelling on both sides. Very little effect on our trenches. Casualties - 2 O.R. wounded. The Battalion was relieved by 3rd/13th Worcestershire Regt. Relief completed at 11.45 pm. Marched to bivouac in Square G.11.c.	Casualties 2. O.R.W.
28th June	Arrived in bivouac 3 A.M. The following officers joined - Lieut. R.F.A.GAVIN, Lieut. J.R. Tuckett, 2nd Lieut. W.P. O'Lone, Lieut. D.Kirkpatrick, (3rd/Bn), 2nd Lieut. M. Ross, 2nd Lieut. K. Ross, & 2nd D.A. La Touche (4th/13n.)	
29th June	In bivouac. Baths taken by Companies at Square H.13.a. Lieut. C.R.B. Dawes to Hospital, sick. Lieut C.J. Wakefield, and	

Army Form C. 2118

WAR DIARY
or
INTELLIGENCE SUMMARY.
(Erase heading not required.)

Instructions regarding War Diaries and Intelligence Summaries are contained in F. S. Regs., Part II. and the Staff Manual respectively. Title pages will be prepared in manuscript.

Hour, Date, Place	Summary of Events and Information	Remarks and References to Appendices
1915	Map Reference – BELGIUM – SHEET 28, 1/40,000	
29 June (cont'd)	and 2nd Lieut. W.E. Andrews proceeded on short leave.	
30 June	In Bivouac. Company Commanders proceeded to inspect the trenches to be taken over. The Commanding Officer and Senior Major (Capt. H.R. Goodman) proceeded later to receive reports of O.C. Coys. Returned to Bivouac at 7 pm.	

J.A. Weir, Major
Commanding 2nd Bn. The R. Irish Rifles.

7th Inf. Bde.
3rd Div.

2nd BATTN. THE ROYAL IRISH RIFLES.

J U L Y

1 9 1 5

WAR DIARY or INTELLIGENCE SUMMARY.

Army Form C. 2118.

(Erase heading not required.)

MAP REFERENCES BELGIUM SHEET 28. 1/40,000

Hour, Date, Place	Summary of Events and Information	Remarks and References to Appendices
1st July 1915	2. Bivouac. Quartermaster Sergeant R.J. O'Gore promoted 2nd Lieut. dated 20th June 1915.	
6 p.m.	The Battalion paraded and marched to the trenches rear HOOGE and relieved the 1st Bn. Wilts. Regt. Casualties 2 W.	
2nd July	In trenches. The enemy fired gas shells on the trenches occupied by "C" Company (C 3 + 4.) in the afternoon. Casualties 1 W. 1 Died from effects of gas poisoning and 8 men affected by gas admitted to hospital. Reinforcement of 193 other ranks joined.	
3rd July	In trenches. Reinforcement of 50 O. Ranks joined. Casualties 1 W.	
4th July	In trenches. Casualties Nil.	
5th July	" " Casualties Nil. The Battalion was relieved by the 1st Bn Wiltshire Regt. and marched to Ennivine. Square G.11.C. Lieut. C. Jusakefield & 2nd Lr. W.G. Andrews rejoined from leave	
6th July	At Bivouac as above. The following message addressed to the Battalion.	

WAR DIARY
or
INTELLIGENCE SUMMARY.

(Erase heading not required.)

Army Form C. 2118.

UNDER 2nd BN. ROYAL IRISH RIFLES.

MAP REFERENCES - BELGIUM - SHEET 28. 1/40,000

Hour, Date, Place	Summary of Events and Information	Remarks and References to Appendices
1915		
6th July 1915 (contd)	Battalion dated 6th July 1915 was received - "The Corps Commander is pleased to hear of the success of your aggressive operations."	
7th July	In bivouac. Lieut. E.A.B. Dawes rejoined from Hospital.	
8th July	" The Battalion marched to the trenches and relieved the 1st/7th Wiltshire Regt.	
9th July	In trenches. Casualties Other Ranks 1 killed, 2 wounded. 2nd Lieut. F.G. Bland died in Hospital from wounds received in the action of June 16th. Reinforcement 60 O/Ranks joined.	
10th July	In trenches. Casualties Other Ranks 1 killed, 4 wounded.	
11th July	" " " Nil. 2nd Lieut. H.E.S. Seth-Smith 4th R.Ir.Rifles joined and posted to B Coy.	
12th July	In trenches. Casualties 2 wounded. The Battalion was relieved by the 1st Bn. Gordon Highlanders, and marched to Bivouac Square G.11.c. 2nd Lt. H. Wearing 4th R.I. Rifles joined & posted to D Coy. Lieut. C.B. Williams & 2nd Lt. R.S. O'Lone proceeded on leave.	

(9 29 6) W 2791 100,000 8/14 H W V Forms/C. 2118/11.

Army Form C. 2118.

WAR DIARY
or
INTELLIGENCE SUMMARY.
(Erase heading not required.)

Instructions regarding War Diaries and Intelligence Summaries are contained in F. S. Regs., Part II. and the Staff Manual respectively. Title pages will be prepared in manuscript.

Hour, Date, Place	Summary of Events and Information	Remarks and references to Appendices
1915	MAP REFERENCES – BELGIUM – SHEET 28. 1/40,000	
13th July	In Bivouac, as above	
14th "	" — 2nd Lieut. W.L. Orr 4th R. Ir. Rifles, joined & posted to C Coy. Casualties 1 O.Rank wounded (Salvage Company YPRES)	
15th "	In Bivouac. Capt G.B. Edwards, R.A.M.C. joined as Medical Officer. Lieut C. Jacobs R.A.M.C. to 7th F. Ambulance for duty.	
16th "	In Bivouac.	
17th "	— " —	
18th "	— " —	
19th "	— " — Lieut C.B. Williams & 2nd Lieut R.L. O'Lone from leave. 2nd Lieut A.A. Raymond & 2nd Lieut O. Fayle proceeded on leave.	
20th "	In Bivouac. Lieut C.B. Dawes proceeded on leave.	
21st "	— " — The Battalion marched to the trenches near ST ELOI & relieved the K.O.S. Borderers. B & C Coys in front line (U 25 & 26, 23 & 24), A & D Coys in support. Casualties 1 W. A draft of 23 other ranks joined.	
22nd "	In trenches. Casualties – Nil.	

WAR DIARY or INTELLIGENCE SUMMARY.

Army Form C. 2118.

(Erase heading not required.)

MAP REFERENCES — BELGIUM — SHEET 28 — 1/40,000.

Hour, Date, Place	Summary of Events and Information	Remarks and references to Appendices
1915		
23rd July	In trenches. — Casualties 1 W. Lieut C.B. Dawes from leave.	
24th "	— " — Casualties. 1 K. 4 W.	
25th "	— " — "A" & "D" Coys relieved "C" & "B" Coys in the fire trenches. B & C Coys withdrew to the Supports. Casualties 2 W.	
26th "	In trenches. The line held by the Battalion was changed and extended. A Coy handed over U23 & 24 to 3rd Worc Regt & relieved 2nd Suffolk Regt in U27. "B" Coy was drawn from the Supports and took over U28 from 2nd Suffolk Regt. D Coy remained in U25 & 26. Casualties 1. Killed.	
27th "	In trenches — Casualties 2. Killed, 2 Wounded	
28th "	— " — " Nil.	
29th "	— " — " 1 Wounded. "C" Coy relieved B Coy in fire trench U28. B Coy withdrew to the Supports.	
30th "	In the trenches. Casualties 1 Killed, 4 wounded. 2nd Lieut J.G. CARUTH, 5th Bn joined and posted to C Coy	
31st "	In trenches. Casualties 3 wounded.	

A.W.— Lieut Col
Comdg. 2nd Bn R. Ir. Rifles

7th Inf.Bde.
3rd Div.

2nd BATTN. THE ROYAL IRISH RIFLES.

A U G U S T

1 9 1 5

2/R Irish Rifles Army Form C. 2118.

WAR DIARY
or
INTELLIGENCE SUMMARY.
(Erase heading not required.)

August 1915

Hour, Date, Place	Summary of Events and Information	Remarks and references to Appendices
1915	MAP REFERENCES - BELGIUM - SHEET 28, 1/40,000	
1st August	In trenches. During the afternoon while our artillery were registering, an enemy shell struck the parapet in U.27. Killing 2nd Lieut. W.E. Andrews & 2nd Lieut A.A. Raymond. Severely wounding Lieut. D. Kirkpatrick, and the Artillery Observing Officer. Also killing 2 and wounding 2, other ranks. Other casualties 5 o.ranks wounded. TOTAL Casualties Killed 2 Officers 2 o.Ranks / Wounded 1 " 7 "	
2nd Aug.	In trenches. Casualties. - 1 Wounded (accidental) 2 L.Sgne by transport wagon. The Battalion was relieved by a detachment of 7th East Yorks Regt. (U.25 + 26), and by the 2nd Suffolk Regt. (U.27, 28, + support dugouts), and marched to bivouac - Square H.25	
3rd Aug.	In bivouac. Lieut C.J. Wakefield to Hospital, sick. 2nd Lieut. R.J. O'Lone took over duties of acting Adjutant. The Battalion paraded at 8.15pm + proceeded to the Support Line	

WAR DIARY or INTELLIGENCE SUMMARY.

Army Form C. 2118.

(Erase heading not required.)

MAP REFERENCES – BELGIUM SHEET 28 1/40,000

Hour, Date, Place 1915.	Summary of Events and Information	Remarks and references to Appendices
3rd Aug (Contd)	Support trenches, X 8, 9, 10 & 11, near ST JEAN. Relieved 1st North Stafford Regt. Casualties 1 Killed.	
4th "	In trenches. Casualties Nil.	
5th "	" — Lieut. G.S. Norman ✠ 19 ORanks joined.	✠ 2nd Royal Irish Rifles
	Casualties – 1 Killed.	
6th "	In trenches. Casualties Nil.	
7th "	" — Lieut. G.S. Norman took over the duties of Adjutant on appointment. The Battalion was relieved by the H.A.C. 11pm and proceeded to the Reserve Dugouts on the Canal Bank, YPRES. Casualties – 2 Wounded.	
8th "	Reserve dugouts as above. Temp. Capt. L.A. Gavin ✠ proceeded on Short Leave. 2nd Lieut. R.A. Roxburgh 3rd Att 1st Rifles joined the Battalion. Casualties Nil.	
9th "	Reserve Dugouts as above. Lieut. C.R.B. Blame ✠ 4th R.I.Rifles, to hospital sick. Lieut H.E. Sett-Smith wounded while in	✠ L.C.J.

WAR DIARY or INTELLIGENCE SUMMARY.

(Erase heading not required.)

Army Form C. 2118.

Hour, Date, Place	Summary of Events and Information	Remarks and references to Appendices
	MAP REFERENCES — BELGIUM SHEET 28 $\frac{1}{40,000}$	
9th August (Anzac) 1915	Charge of a digging party. 2nd Lieut L.G.M. Bennett to Hospital Sick. Casualties Officer 1	
10th "	Reserve Dugouts as above. Draft 30 Other Ranks joined the Battalion. Casualties 1	
11th "	Reserve Dugouts as above. Battalion relieved 1ST WILTS in trenches near ST JEAN - (part of one line running through WEILTJE. 2ND Lieut Hill and 2nd Lieut Anderson - 9th Argyll and Sutherland Highlanders attached to the Battalion for 148 hrs instruction in trench Warfare. Casualties Nil.	
12th "	In trenches as above. Quiet day. Slight shelling by Germans directed on our trenches. No damage done. Casualties Nil	
13th "	Trenches as above. Working party of C. Coy Shelled by day. 2 Germans Killed. Casualties Nil	
14th "	In trenches as above. Quiet day. 1 German Killed by our Snipers. Casualties Nil	

WAR DIARY or INTELLIGENCE SUMMARY

Army Form C. 2118.

MAP REFERENCES – BELGIUM – SHEET 28 1/40,000

Hour, Date, Place	Summary of Events and Information	Remarks and references to Appendices

15th August 1915
In trenches as above. Lieut K Ross and patrol met German patrol about 300x in front of our trenches. One German was killed and two captured. They belonged to 236 Regt. XXVI Reserve Army Corps. Our patrol had no casualties. Casualties 2 Wounded. (night 15/16)

16th
In trenches as above. Lieut C Wakefield injured from hospital. Quiet day, though some slight shelling. Casualties 5 Wounded.

17th
In trenches as above. Quiet day. 2 Germans killed by our snipers. Casualties 1 Wounded.

18th
In trenches as above. Quiet day. Slight shelling. Casualties Nil.

19th
In trenches as above. Quiet day. Slight shelling. One German killed by our sniper. Relieved about 11.15 p.m. by 2nd YORK and LANCS Regt. Went to bivouac in H 25 D. Casualties killed 10 Wounded.

J.S.

WAR DIARY
or
INTELLIGENCE SUMMARY.
(Erase heading not required.)

Army Form C. 2118.

Hour, Date, Place 1915	Summary of Events and Information	Remarks and references to Appendices
	MAP REFERENCES — BELGIUM — SHEET 28 — 1/40,000	
20th August	In bivouac in H25D. Battalion ready to move off at one hour's notice. "A" Coy inlying piquet ready to move off at ½ hour's notice. Casualties Nil	Lieut M MacKenzie R.A.M.C relieved Capt G W Edwards R.A.M.C as M.O. to the bn.
21st "	In bivouac as above. Battalion ready to move off at one hour's notice. "B" Coy inlying piquet ready to move off at ½ hour's notice. Casualties Nil. Capt (Temp) W.P. Sloane proceeded on short leave.	
22nd "	In bivouac as above. Battalion ready to move off at one hour's notice. "C" Coy inlying piquet ready to move off at ½ hour's notice. 1 Officer and 1 Platoon detailed as aeroplane guard. Casualties Nil. Lt S. Bell rejoined and posted to D Company	
23rd "	In bivouac as above. Bn on duty. Casualties Nil	
24th "	In bivouac as above. Bn proceed at 7pm and marched to YPRES, relieving 2nd LEINSTER Regt. A, B & D Coys in Ramparts, C Coy in dugouts. S bank of ZILLEBEKE LAKE	

J.C.

WAR DIARY or INTELLIGENCE SUMMARY

Army Form C. 2118.

(Erase heading not required.)

Summary of Events and Information

MAP REFERENCES - BELGIUM - SHEET 28 1/40,000

Hour, Date, Place 1915		Remarks and references to Appendices
24th August (Cont)	Lieuts E WORKMAN - E GRIBBEN and W.E. MORTON 5th Royal Irish Rifles joined battalion - having transferred from 1st YORK and LANCS Regt.	
25th "	In Dugout - as above. About six shells fell near dugouts. Casualties - 1 Killed 5 Wounded	
26th "	Quiet day in Ramparts. Casualties Nil.	
27th "	In Ramparts as above. Relieved 1st WILTS in trenches at HOOGE. Reached from Ramparts 8 pm. Some activity during relief on part of Germans who attempted by bombing to prevent 1st WILTS and 2nd S.LANCS from driving 6 trench in front of CHATEAU Stables the Bombers retaliated successfully. Casualties 1 wounded.	
28th "	In trenches as above. Some heavy shelling by enemy in neighbourhood of CRATER, lasting about	

WAR DIARY or INTELLIGENCE SUMMARY

Army Form C. 2118.

MAP REFERENCES - BELGIUM - SHEET 28 1/40,000

About half an hour. Casualties Capt WILLIAMS KILLED
 2 other ranks "
 LT. C.W. WAKEFIELD WOUNDED
 other ranks 17

During night 28th/29th Some activity on part of German snipers which interfered with working parties near craters.
In trenches as above
Slight shelling about 5 a.m. Otherwise quiet day
During night 29th/30th machine gun(August connected up a new trench behind (S side) of stables at HOOGE held by 3rd WORCESTERS.
LT. G.W. CALVERLEY 2nd R.I. Rifles rejoined
Casualties 6 wounded.
In trenches as above. Quiet day. Bn. relieved by 1st WILTS and marched to bivouac H.22.c. Casualties 5 wounded

Army Form C. 2118.

WAR DIARY
or
INTELLIGENCE SUMMARY.
(Erase heading not required.)

Instructions regarding War Diaries and Intelligence Summaries are contained in F. S. Regs., Part II. and the Staff Manual respectively. Title pages will be prepared in manuscript.

Hour, Date, Place	Summary of Events and Information	Remarks and references to Appendices
	MAP REFERENCES - BELGIUM - SHEET 28 - 1/40,000	
31st August	In bivouac H 22 c Casualties Nil	
1st Septr		

L. C. Sprague Major
Comdg 2/R. Irish Rifles
19. 10. 15.

7th Inf.Bde.
3rd Div.

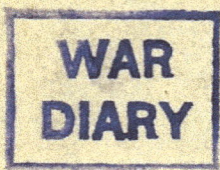

2nd BATTN. THE ROYAL IRISH RIFLES.

S E P T E M B E R

1 9 1 5

Attached:

Trench Map.

WAR DIARY
or
INTELLIGENCE SUMMARY.

(Erase heading not required.)

Army Form C. 2118.

Hour, Date, Place	Summary of Events and Information	Remarks and references to Appendices
1915	MAP REFERENCES - BELGIUM - SHEET 28 - 1/40,000	
1st September	In bivouac H.22.c. No Casualties.	
2nd "	In bivouac H.22.c. No Casualties. Very wet weather	
3rd "	In bivouac H.22.c. Very wet. Paraded at 6.30 pm. and relieved 1st WILTSHIRE REGT in trenches at HOOGE. Casualties 1 wounded	
4th "	In trenches as above. From 4.30am - 5am. and from 10.30am to 11.30am. our heavy and light artillery bombarded enemy's trenches in front and E. and W. of CRATER. Enemy retaliated with heavy and light guns. Casualties LT W.E. MORTON 5th R.I. Rifles killed. Other ranks 1 KILLED 16 WOUNDED	
5th "	Heavy rain nearly all day. 37th Reinforcement of 20 other ranks joined the battalion. Night 4th/5th Quiet. Our artillery cohebre bombarded enemy's trenches from 4.40am - 5am and 12.5pm - 12.55pm. J.C.J.	

WAR DIARY or INTELLIGENCE SUMMARY

Army Form C. 2118.

MAP REFERENCES – BELGIUM – SHEET 28 – 1/40,000

Hour, Date, Place	Summary of Events and Information	Remarks and references to Appendices

5th September (Cont.) — Germans retaliated, damaging dugouts in CRATER considerably. Heavy rain during the day. Casualties 2 killed 9 wounded. Captain H.E. GIFFORD 2nd Royal Irish Rifles rejoined from 60th Bde. 2nd Lieut R.A. ROSSBOROUGH 3rd Royal Irish Rifles to hospital sick.

6th — In trenches as above. Night 5th/6th Quiet. Some rain during day. Desultory shelling by both sides during day. Casualties Officers Lt. Col. G.A. WEIR – 3rd Dragoons – Commanding 2nd Royal Irish Rifles slightly wounded, and remained at duty. Other ranks 4 wounded. B.M. Gunners joined.

7th — In trenches as above. Quiet day. Weather fine. Very little shelling. 2nd Lieut. H.W. WEAVING, 4th Royal Irish Rifles to hospital sick. Casualties 1 wounded.

8th — In trenches as above. Quiet day. Patrols out at night 8th/9th. Rather German bombing post of 16 bombs. Casualties 5 wounded. 2nd LT. O. FAYLE 4th R.I. Rifles transferred to 3rd Coy R.E. (Authy a/g Nº A/6959 dated 8.9.15)

J.C.B.

WAR DIARY or INTELLIGENCE SUMMARY.

(Erase heading not required.)

Army Form C. 2118.

Summary of Events and Information

MAP REFERENCES - BELGIUM - SHEET 28 - 1/40,000

Hour, Date, Place 1915		Remarks and references to Appendices
9th September	In trenches as above. Quiet day. Relieved in trenches by 1/5 WILTSHIRE REGT. and went to Ramparts in YPRES. Casualties 5 wounded.	
10th "	In Ramparts. Quiet day. Casualties 1 killed 1 wounded.	
11th "	In Ramparts as above. Quiet day. Casualties 1 wounded.	
12th "	In Ramparts as above. Quiet day. Relieved about 8.30 p.m. by 4/5 MIDDLESEX REGT. and marched to bivouac G 17 D 3.6	Casualties Nil
13th "	In bivouac as above. Casualties Nil	
14th "	In bivouac as above. Casualties 1 accidentally wounded partaking hooking.	
15th "	2nd LT. O. FAYLE left Bn. to join 3rd Coy R.E. In bivouac as above. Draft 16 other ranks arrived. G.O.C.in.C. 2nd Army inspected Bn. at 3.55 p.m. Casualties Nil.	
16th "	In bivouac as above.	
17th "	In bivouac as above.	
18th "	In bivouac as above. Casualties 1 wounded on working party.	

D.C.

WAR DIARY or INTELLIGENCE SUMMARY.

Army Form C. 2118.

(Erase heading not required.)

Hour, Date, Place	Summary of Events and Information	Remarks and references to Appendices
1915	MAP REFERENCE - BELGIUM - SHEET 28 - 1/40,000	
September 19th	In bivouac G.17.C. as above. Casualties Nil	
20th	In bivouac as above. Casualties Nil	
21st	In bivouac as above. Casualties Nil. 2nd Lieut. C.K. EDWARDS 4/Royal Irish Rifles joined.	
22nd	In bivouac as above. One man accidentally wounded. Captain Kempton 2/Lt Wilkins & Lt Tuckett rejoined after leave. Officers joined:- Capt. D.H. KELLY 3/Royal Inniskilling Fusrs Capt. W. CUPPLES 3/Royal Inniskilling Fusrs Captain H.N. YOUNG (Reporter) Royal Inniskilling Fusrs.	
23rd	Othermands 20. In bivouac as above. Bn. paraded 5.30 p.m. and marched to bivouac near KRUISTRAAT. Strength of Bn. 650 Rifles + 96 others (Signallers-orderlies-servants etc) Captain H.G.C. PERRY-AYSCOUGH 4/Connaught Rangers and LT. F.H. BETHELL 3/Connaught Rangers joined.	
24th	In bivouac as above. Operation Orders and plan	

WAR DIARY or INTELLIGENCE SUMMARY

Army Form C. 2118.

Hour, Date, Place	Summary of Events and Information	Remarks and references to Appendices
1915	MAP REFERENCES – BELGIUM – SHEET 28 – $\frac{1}{40000}$	
September 24th (Cont)	of impending attack finally discussed. The following are extracts from Operation Order No 21 by Lt Col G.A. WEIR 3rd D.G. Cmdg 2nd Royal Irish Rifles dated 24th Sept 1915. "Y Corps with XIV Division attacked hill attack and occupy the front J19a.6.8 to I12a.0.4. The front allotted to 2nd Royal Irish Rifles is from I12d.4.1 to front on BELLEWARDE LAKE due EAST from I12a.0.4. B and D Companies will carry out the assault and assemble in trenches C5, C6, C7. Five minutes before bombardment ceases these Companies will leave their trenches and deploy opposite their front of attack. The night of 23rd-24th in touch with "B" Coy will be directed on I18G.2.9 – I12a.2.0 – 31.41 – in touch with 2nd South Lancashire Regt. The left of D Company will be directed on I12C.G.3 – I12a.0.4. BELLEWARDE LAKE in touch with 5th Shropshire L.I. XIV Division. Signal for the assault will be the explosion of the second mine	REF. attached { Special trench map and Sheet 28 $\frac{1}{40000}$ } J.C.

WAR DIARY
or
INTELLIGENCE SUMMARY.
(Erase heading not required.)

Army Form C. 2118.

Hour, Date, Place	Summary of Events and Information	Remarks and references to Appendices
1915	MAP REFERENCES - BELGIUM SHEET 28 1/40,000	
24th September (Cont)	The line finally to be consolidated will be directed on I.12.d.4.1. – 3.1. – point on BELLEWARDE LAKE East D on joining up with 2/ South Lancashire Regt on the right towards I.18.b.6.9. and with 5th Shropshire L.I. on the left towards I.12.d.1.6. C Company will be in support and will occupy C.5, C.6 and C.7 as soon as B and D Companies move out. Two platoons representing B Company and two platoons representing D Company. A Company will be in Reserve and will extend and occupy C Companys assembly trenches with two platoons when C Company moves forward. Bn paraded 7.10 pm. and marched to trenches at HOOGE. Relieved H.A.C. in trenches C.5, C.6 and C.7 at 11.20 pm. Bn Adgers in Dugout under MENIN ROAD I.18.a.3.6.	

WAR DIARY
or
INTELLIGENCE SUMMARY.
(Erase heading not required.)

Army Form C. 2118.

Hour, Date, Place	Summary of Events and Information	Remarks and references to Appendices
1915	MAP REFERENCES - BELGIUM SHEET 28 1/40,000	
September 25th	2 minutes as above. Our artillery bombarded the front to be attacked from 3.50 am until 4.20 am - lifting their fire gradually from the front line to support line commencing at 4.50 am. Smoke mines were exposed on right - first pair at 4.19 am, second pair at 4.19½ am. The assault was delivered at 4.19½ am. At 4.14 am the attacking companies crossed the parapet and deployed about 30 yards in front in a line with the island and which swung out from C6. Each company had 2 platoons in the front line and 2 platoons in the second line. The second line was just in front of the parapet. Six sections of bombers and two machine guns accompanied the attack. Between 29 and Q1 the attack reached the German second line, and occupied it with little opposition, but no bombers reached the objective and	4.25 am

WAR DIARY
or
INTELLIGENCE SUMMARY.
(Erase heading not required.)

Army Form C. 2118.

Hour, Date, Place	Summary of Events and Information	Remarks and references to Appendices
1915	MAP REFERENCES - BELGIUM - SHEET 28 $\frac{1}{40000}$	
September 26 (cont)	A Bomb attack by the enemy forced those who had reached it to retire to the German front line, where our Officer and some slaves were held on till dark. Squares 29 and between 91-93. The attack was held up by rifle and machine gun fire, and the men took what cover they could in shell holes close up to the German lines. Some of them rejoined after dark. At about 4.30 A.m. C Coy in Support went up to reinforce the attacking companies, who were seen to have retaken the enemy's line. This Company however met with heavy rifle and machine gun fire, and few if any succeeded in reaching the enemy's trenches. "A" Company then moved up and occupied our front line trenches. At about 6 A.m. some of our men were seen still be seen in the enemy's trenches, but after that hour nothing further could be seen of them.	

WAR DIARY
or
INTELLIGENCE SUMMARY.

(Erase heading not required.)

Army Form C. 2118.

Hour, Date, Place	Summary of Events and Information	Remarks and references to Appendices
	MAP REFERENCES - BELGIUM - SHEET 28 - 1/40,000	
September 25th 10/15 (Cont)	and although patrols & volunteers to go forward & find out what was going on in front, none succeeded in getting definite information, and headquarters remained in doubt as to the actual situation till evening. None of the Dispatches who accompanied the attack succeeded in getting back and messages & runners sent to enquire and search until dawn. The situation remained unchanged until dawn, when those of the attacking Companies, who were able, rejoined. The total Casualties were about 15 Officers and three hundred and fifty other ranks. One Machine Gun reached the German first line & Lewis Guns about 60, but the teams were either killed or captured, and the few who found shelter in a hole who came back from the German front line, he discharged it with the butt of his rifle before retiring at night. The attack was carried out	

WAR DIARY
or
INTELLIGENCE SUMMARY.

(Erase heading not required.)

Army Form C. 2118.

Hour, Date, Place	Summary of Events and Information	Remarks and references to Appendices
	MAP REFERENCES - BELGIUM - SHEET 28 $\frac{1}{10,000}$	
September 25th (cont) 1915	with the greatest determination and gallantry, and the Reserve Company, after it[?] saw that the attack had been in the Main unsuccessful, was still eager to be allowed to join in. A Company of 1st Wilts moved up into Reserve in place of 'A' Company. About midnight 25th/26th 1st Wilts commenced relief and our relief was completed at 2.15 am 26th. Casualties. Officers Killed:- LT. AVERILLE D. LA TOUCHE 5th Royal Irish Rifles. 2ND LT. WALTER LESLIE ORR 4th Royal Irish Rifles. 2ND LT. JAMES GORDON CARUTH 5th Royal Irish Rifles. 2ND LT. MELBOURNE ROSS 4th Royal Irish Rifles. WOUNDED CAPTAIN WILLIAM CUPPLES 3rd Royal Inniskilling Fusiliers. CAPTAIN HERBERT NEWTON YOUNG R. Inniskilling Fusiliers (Regular?)C.S.	

WAR DIARY
or
INTELLIGENCE SUMMARY.
(Erase heading not required.)

Army Form C. 2118.

Hour, Date, Place	Summary of Events and Information	Remarks and references to Appendices
1915	MAP REFERENCES - BELGIUM - SHEET 28 - 1/40,000	
25th September (Cont)	WOUNDED (Cont) LT. THOMAS HENRY ~~CALVERLEY~~ IVEY 2ND Royal Irish Rifles.	
	LT. GEOFFREY WALTER CALVERLEY 2ND Royal Irish Rifles.	
	LT. JOHN REGINALD TUCKETT - 2ND Royal Irish Rifles.	
	WOUNDED and MISSING.	
	CAPT. HENRY GEORGE CHARLES PERRY-AYSCOUGH 4th Connaught Rangers	
	T/CAPT. WALTER PERCY O'LONE - 2ND Royal Irish Rifles.	
	T/CAPT. ROBERT FITZ-AUSTIN GAVIN - 2ND Royal Irish Rifles.	
	2ND LT. KENNETH ROSS - 4th Royal Irish Rifles.	
	MISSING	
	LT. FRANK HARRY BETHEL - 3rd Connaught Rangers	
	WOUNDED SLIGHTLY (at duty)	
	2ND LT. S BELL	
	OTHER RANKS. Killed 46 Wounded 140 Missing 150 Wounded + Missing 26 M.G. and team lost	

WAR DIARY
or
INTELLIGENCE SUMMARY.
(Erase heading not required.)

Army Form C. 2118.

Place	Date	Summary of Events and Information	Remarks and references to Appendices
MAP REFERENCES - BELGIUM - SHEET 28 - 1/40,000			
	26th	In Bivouac G.17.D.3.6. No Casualties. 2nd LT. H.M. ANDERSON 18 (London Irish Rifles joined) 2nd LT. G.J.M. BENNET rejoined from hospital (4 R.I. Rifles)	
	27th	In Bivouac as above. I Corps Commander came about 10 a.m. and addressed the troops. Congratulating them on their gallant conduct. Casualties Nil	
	28th	In Bivouac as above. Casualties Nil	
	29th	In Bivouac as above. Casualties Nil. LT. MACKENZIE - R.A.M.C. to England on leave. Retired as {LT. FREW. R.A.M.C.	
	30th	In Bivouac as above. Casualties Nil	

L.C. Sprague Major.
Comdg 2/R Irish Rifles
19.10.15.

P.A

War diary
2/ R. Irish Rifles

August 1914
Sept. 1914
respectively

7th Inf.Bde.
3rd Div.

Battn. transferred
with Bde. to 25th
Div. 18.10.15.

Battn. transferred
to 74th Inf.Bde.
25th Div. 26.10.15.

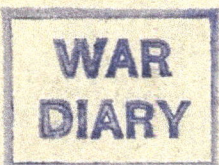

2nd BATTN. THE ROYAL IRISH RIFLES.

O C T O B E R

1 9 1 5

WAR DIARY
or
INTELLIGENCE SUMMARY.
(Erase heading not required.)

Army Form C. 2118

Hour, Date, Place	Summary of Events and Information	Remarks and references to Appendices
1915	MAP REFERENCES - BELGIUM - SHEET 28 1/40,000	
October 1st.	In bivouac as above. Battalion paraded at 5 p.m. and marched via KRUISSTRAAT to trenches in front of ARMAGH WOOD T30c. relieving 1/4 LINCOLN RGT. Relief complete about 2 am on 2nd. Casualties nil. Captain F.M.S. GIBSON 3rd Connaught Rangers and LT. D.B. de ALVAREZ BORCHARDS 4th Connaught Rangers joined.	
2nd	In trenches as above. Quiet day except in the late afternoon Enemy's Minnenwerfer and light field gun shelled the trenches in one Batt. for ½ quarter of an hour. Casualties - Capt. F.M.S. GIBSON 3/Connaught Rangers - 2nd LT. A.E. KEMP 2nd R.I. Rifles and LT. D.T.C. FREW - R.A.M.C (remained at duty) Wounded. Other ranks 1 killed 4 wounded. Draft 19 O Ranks joined.	[signatures]

WAR DIARY or INTELLIGENCE SUMMARY

Army Form C. 2118

MAP REFERENCES - BELGIUM - SHEET 28 1/40,000

Hour, Date, Place	Summary of Events and Information	Remarks
October 3rd 1915	In trenches as above. Quiet day except for slight shelling with light field gun and a few minenwerfer. Enemy Casualties nil.	
4th	In trenches as above. Quiet day except for enemy's light field guns and minenwerfer which shelled for a little while about 5 pm. Casualties 5 wounded. Following Officers joined the Battalion. LT. D.H. STOKER 4/R.I. Regiment 2LT. E.D. PRICE 3/R.I. Regiment 2LT. T. BURTON FORSTER 3/R.I. Regiment 2LT. F.J. KING 4/R.I. Regiment and 161 Other ranks.	
5th	In trenches as above. Three Officers of Norfolks attached to the Bn. for instruction. Casualties 5 wounded. LT. D.H. STOKER 4/R.I. Regiment to Hospital sick. Quiet day, except for usual slight shelling by enemy 77 M.M. field gun and minenwerfer.	L.C. Sprague Major ?? 2/R Irish Rifles

WAR DIARY
or
INTELLIGENCE SUMMARY.
(Erase heading not required.)

Army Form C. 2118

Hour, Date, Place	Summary of Events and Information	Remarks and references to Appendices
1915	MAP REFERENCES - BELGIUM - SHEET 28 1/40,000	
October 6th.	In trenches as above. Quiet day. 1½ Corp - M.G. Section - M.O. - Stretcher bearers and bombers of 9th returned. Arrived about 11.30 p.m. for instruction - 3 Officers and 267 other ranks altogether. Casualties Nil	
7th.	In trenches as above - Quiet day, except for usual slight shelling by enemy 77 M.M. field gun and minenwerfer. Casualties 3 wounded. Following Officers joined the Battalion. LT. J.A. STEWART 3/R.I. Rifles. LT. W.P. MOSS 3/R.I. Rifles - LT. W.C. McCONNELL 3/R.I. Rifles - 2 LT. F.K. WHITE R.I. Rifles. Also 43 other ranks.	
8th	In trenches as above. Quiet day except for usual slight shelling as above. LT FREW R.A.M.C. returned to 9th Field Ambulance. LT. MACKENZIE returned from leave. Casualties 2 wounded. 9th Norfolks relieved by Munsters 1½ Corp. altogether 3 Officers 248 O.R.	1 - C. Sprague Major R. Irish Rifles Cmdg 9/R. Irish Rifles

WAR DIARY
or
INTELLIGENCE SUMMARY.
(Erase heading not required.)

Army Form C. 2118

Instructions regarding War Diaries and Intelligence Summaries are contained in F. S. Regs., Part II. and the Staff Manual respectively. Title pages will be prepared in manuscript.

MAP REFERENCES — BELGIUM — SHEET 28 1/40,000

Hour, Date, Place 1915	Summary of Events and Information	Remarks and references to Appendices
October 9th	In trenches as above. Quiet day. Usual slight shelling as above. Casualties 4 wounded. 10 Cadets from School of Instruction arrived for 24 hours instruction.	
10th	In trenches as above. Quiet day. Usual slight shelling – also a few high explosive shells fired by enemy. 7" M.H. field gun and minenwerfer. Casualties 2 wounded. The 10 Cadets departed at 5 pm.	
11th	Amp all 9/ Norfolks left about 6.30 pm. In trenches as above. Quiet day. Lt. Col. G. A. WEIR 3rd D.G. ordered to command 8th Infantry Brigade 1st Corps – with temporary rank of Brigadier General. He left about 3 pm. Casualties 2 killed 2 wounded.	
12th	In trenches as above. Quiet day. Bn. relieved about 10.30 pm by 1st H.A.C. And marched to Busseme. G7 14 c 3.6. Casualties nil.	

T. C. Spurgeon Major
Comdg 9/R. Irish Rifles

WAR DIARY
or
INTELLIGENCE SUMMARY.
(Erase heading not required.)

Army Form C. 2118

Instructions regarding War Diaries and Intelligence Summaries are contained in F. S. Regs., Part II. and the Staff Manual respectively. Title pages will be prepared in manuscript.

Hour, Date, Place	Summary of Events and Information	Remarks and references to Appendices
1915	MAP REFERENCES – BELGIUM – SHEET 28 1/40000	
October 13th	In bivouac G.17.c.3.6. Quiet day. No Casualties.	
14th	In bivouac as above. About 12 noon G.O.C. III Div. addressed the troops – congratulating them on their gallant conduct and magnificent Bre[re]ull to the Bn. as they were leaving his Command, as the 7th Brigade was to form from the 25th Division, as it had been decided to mix the new units with the New Br. parties 2.30 p.m. and marched via POPERINGHE to L.22.a.5.2 (Map ref. Sheet 27/40000) Casualties Nil. Major L.C. SPRAGUE Royal Irish Rifles joined the battalion and took over Command.	2ND LT. T.S. JENKINSON 5th Royal Irish Fusiliers and 2ND LT. T.J. THOMPSON 4th R.I. Fusiliers joined the battalion 13.10.15
15th	In bivouac L.22.a.5.2. Draft O. Ranks 16 Arrived Casualties Nil	
16th	In bivouac as above. Bn. paraded at 5.50 p.m. and marched via ABEELE – GODEWAERSVELDE	Ref Map BELGIUM HAZEBROUCK 5A 1/100,000

L/C[?] Sprague Maj
Lt. Col. I/R. Irish Rifles

WAR DIARY
or
INTELLIGENCE SUMMARY.
(Erase heading not required.)

Army Form C. 2118

Hour, Date, Place	Summary of Events and Information	Remarks and references to Appendices
1915	MAP REFERENCES - BELGIUM (HAZEBROUCK 5A) 1/100,000	
October 16 (cont)	- FLETRE - STRAZEELE to MERRIS. The battalion arrived about 11.30 pm and billeted in farm houses just N.E. of MERRIS in 2nd Corps area. Casualties Nil	
17th	In billets as above.	
18th	In billets as above.	
19th	In billets as above.	
20th	In billets as above. Draft of 12 other ranks arrived.	
21st	In billets as above. G.O.C. 2nd Corps addressed the Bn.	
22nd	In billets as above.	
23rd	In billets as above.	
24th	In billets as above. G.O.C. XXV Division inspected the Battalion and welcomed it into his division.	
25th	In billets as above. Battalion paraded at 9 am and marched via OULTERSTEEN to BAILLEUL where Battalion billeted.	
26th	In billets as above. Battalion paraded 8 am and	

Lindsay Major
2/R Irish Rifles

WAR DIARY
or
INTELLIGENCE SUMMARY.
(Erase heading not required.)

Army Form C. 2118.

Hour, Date, Place	Summary of Events and Information	Remarks and references to Appendices
1915	MAP REFERENCES - BELGIUM and FRANCE - Sheets 28 and 36 40,000	
26th October (cont)	Marched from BALLEUL by Companies at 10 minute intervals to LE BIZET. First Company arrived about 11 am where it and remainder of the Battalion billetted.	
27th	2 billets as above. Battalion proceeded to the trenches during afternoon and evening, commencing at 4 pm. Trenches occupied here at LE TOUQUET. Casualties Nil	} relieved 13th Cheshire Regt.
28th	Draft of 11 other ranks joined the battalion just night. In trenches as above. Very quiet day. Casualties Nil	
29th	In trenches as above. Very quiet day. Casualties Nil 2nd LIEUT. C.H.W. DARLING 3rd Royal Irish Rifles joined the battalion	
30th	In trenches as above. Quiet during the day, but at 5 pm our trench mortar at LE TOUQUET fires at enemy. Slight retaliation on part of Germans. Casualties Nil	2 L. Sprague transf'd to hospital Oct [?] 2/R. In. Rgt

Captain H.R.H. IRELAND 3/Jhinstr Regt. (attached)

Army Form C. 2118

WAR DIARY
or
INTELLIGENCE SUMMARY.
(Erase heading not required.)

Instructions regarding War Diaries and Intelligence Summaries are contained in F. S. Regs., Part II. and the Staff Manual respectively. Title pages will be prepared in manuscript.

Hour, Date, Place	Summary of Events and Information	Remarks and references to Appendices
1915	MAP REFERENCES = BELGIUM and FRANCE - Sheet 36	40,000
October 31ST	2 trenches as above. Very quiet day. At night our patrols went out, but discovered nothing of importance. Casualties Nil.	

L. Spoor Major
Cmdg 2 R Irish Rif

www.ingramcontent.com/pod-product-compliance
Lightning Source LLC
Chambersburg PA
CBHW081405160426
43193CB00013B/2112